Deep Citizenship

Paul Barry Clarke

Pluto Press

LONDON · CHICAGO, IL.

First published 1996 by Pluto Press
345 Archway Road, London N6 5AA
and 1436 West Randolph,
Chicago, Illinois 60607, USA

ISBN 0 7453 1102 4 hbk

British Library Cataloguing in Publication Data
A catalogue record for this book is available from
the British Library

Library of Congress Cataloging in Publication Data
Clarke, Paul A. B., 1946–
    Deep citizenship/Paul Barry Clarke
        p.   cm.
    Includes bibliographical references and index.
    ISBN 0–7453–1102–4 (hbk.)
    1. Citizenship. 2. Political participation. I. Title.
JF801.C577   1996
323.6—dc20   95–52758
                                                              CIP

Designed and produced for Pluto Press by
Chase Production Services, Chipping Norton, OX7 5QR
Typeset from disk by Stanford DTP Services, Milton Keynes
Printed in the EC by T.J. Press, Padstow

Contents

Acknowledgements

There is a sense in which acknowledgements are unnecessary. Generally the people involved well know their contribution. Why then acknowledgements?

In this case some of the people involved do not know their contribution. First, the management at Park Coppice who had some general sense of what I was up to during the summer of 1995 and who did their best to respect the requests for peace and quiet. It was in that wonderfully inspiring atmosphere that the book was drafted. Second, Rowan and Tristan do not know yet their contribution except in the most general way. They do know that the categories of academic work and children do not couple well and that their contribution to the former was to keep the latter out of the way. They did this with surprising humour and understanding beyond their years. I hope the lesson in the Protestant work ethic was of about the right amount, neither too much nor too little.

Those who do know that they have made a contribution are, once again, Ildi who pushed me hard and tolerated the consequences, and my editorial director Anne Beech who prodded me hard and incisively on the original manuscript. Both know of their contribution, but neither know the full extent of it. I have been fortunate in the good humoured scepticism my colleagues and graduate students have brought to my observations. I am again conscious of the remarkable international flavour of the research environment offered by the University of Essex. That environment is second to none both in quality and in breadth.

Ultimately of course any errors in the book are mine and taking responsibility for the mistakes one makes is itself an aspect of deep citizenship.

Introduction

The idea of deep citizenship that I propose here is part of a wider argument for radical post-liberal democratic politics. By that I take it that the liberal and democratic tradition of thought offers much that can yet be delivered in the way of individual and shared participation both in the practice of one's own life and in shaping the conditions of that life. The twin concepts within which that expectation could be met are autonomy and citizenship. Although it is the latter concept that I emphasise here these concepts cannot be entirely separated for they are two closely related aspects of political life. To be autonomous is to act for reasons of one's own and to take responsibility for those actions. To act as a citizen, as that is widely understood, is to use that independence in the public domain and orient it towards the common good. This universal dimension of political action is a good frequently expressed and re-expressed within the Western tradition of thought and one that I re-assert.

To be political in the sense in which I construe that term is a good in itself, and the broader mechanism within which it is acted out is through citizenship and the practice of the civic virtues. What I will argue is that for all the promise contained within the political outlook the public domain, as traditionally conceived, has failed to offer adequate opportunity for political action and for the practice of the civic virtues. Relatedly the conception of a common good has also failed and been replaced by a wide variety of differing goods.

A major response to that has been to turn away from all perfectionisms and argue instead for a procedural liberalism in which the right precedes the good and which permits a variety of competing goods to be attained within a broadly neutral framework. There are a number of effects of this switch in emphasis from the classic to the modern model, one of which is to regard the principal attainment of life goals as contained within the private domain. The corollary of that is to remove the conception that acting politically is a good in itself as opposed to a means to some other end. The combined effect of these failures has resulted in a conception of citizenship which is at best irrelevant to the lives of people and at worst distorting, limited and shallow.

1

I shall argue that this problem in the conception of citizenship, while one of recent note, is not of recent origin nor is it merely a surface phenomenon. The problems with citizenship go right to the historical and philosophical foundations of that concept: citizenship too often emasculates and enervates rather than emancipates and energises. It supports a conception of democracy that remains less as unfinished business than as business scarcely started, and it invokes a conception of politics that is exclusive rather than inclusive. Against this backdrop the promises of empowerment, autonomy, liberation, freedom and individual self-responsibility that abound in contemporary political language range between the hypocritical and the hollow.

This might seem like grounds for pessimism with respect to the ideas and the practice of citizenship. I shall argue to the contrary that the conditions which have permitted the identification of the problem of citizenship are also conditions that can be utilised to revitalise that concept and turn it to significant and meaningful concerns in the shared lives of people. Correcting the problems surrounding citizenship concepts requires a radical rethink across a whole range of interrelated areas. It requires the re-conceptualisation of some central ideas which are embedded in common parlance and common practice to such an extent that their meaning and use are taken for granted. That rethink is necessary, difficult and radical. It is necessary for the sense of crisis that is found at the end of the millennium needs to be replaced by a mood of optimism. It is difficult for it means uncovering the foundations of some unfortunate central political concepts and practices which are embedded in culture and in consciousness. It is radical for it takes citizenship, which is currently centred on the state, and de-centres it, moving it away from the state; as it does this so it alters modern conceptions of politics. If the vocabulary of empowerment, autonomy, liberation, freedom and individual self-responsibility that abounds in contemporary political language is to seem less than hypocritical or hollow, and if the promises contained within those concepts are to be met, then a radical re-conceptualisation of politics and of the political virtues is required.

The case I argue is based on the conditions that have led to the recognition of the weakness of current conceptions of citizenship. It is post-liberal not anti-liberal. The liberal tradition of thought offers much that is of value and much that needs little defence, while its failures, as I present them, are failures in its own terms – of a failure to maintain its own potential.

I will point up a number of areas in which the promise of liberalism has not been fully maintained but principal among them rests, first, on a confusion arising from the belief that a failure to identify a single common good implies an end to all shared goods and, second, that a failure of clarity in the boundaries of the public domain means an end to the public domain. I shall argue that it offers instead the opportunity of a growth in the number of public domains. Taken together this re-conceptualisation of liberalism as post-liberalism offers an enhanced opportunity to exercise autonomy, reclaim politics and orient actions towards a variety of shared concerns in a variety of objects and towards a variety of publics.

Such concerns expand and interlock with the concerns of other publics. The expansion of the circles of concern takes in self, others and world, both social and natural. This autonomous action oriented towards shared common goods in a variety of interlocking publics is the foundation of deep citizenship and the renewed opportunity for the practice of the best of the civic virtues. The argument I propose transcends the debate between liberalism and communitarianism or between liberalism and Marxism. I take the view that some central values of liberalism can be combined with the practice of the civic virtues. Such a combination can permit that enlargement of mind characteristic of a civic and humane outlook and which is required for and supportive of politics and citizenship.

The argument I offer is perfectionist. I continue a long line of thought that acting politically is a good in itself and is even distinctively human. That term is understood in the Western tradition of thought, but is not confined to that tradition, and I offer an argument for an expanded and non-Western humanism. The starting idea is best expressed in Dante's conception of *politizare,* of being political for its own sake and for its own delight. A perfectionism of that kind does not prescribe content and so does not propose a single good. Nor does it take it that the good is prior to the right or the right prior to the good. Such prioritising, which was characteristic of the liberal-communitarian debate, seems to me to be mistaken in a number of ways.

Suffice for now to note that I regard it as a major function of the constitutional and liberal democratic state to protect and provide security of civil association. While accepting that, I also regard it as a function of the constitutional and liberal democratic state to protect the spaces and contexts within which new politics and new political spaces can arise. This has clear pro-active educational and welfare implications. If empowerment is to be meaningful it has to be backed by the means to bring it about. This new politics provides the opportunity for *politizare,* and the practice of the civic virtues. If a shorthand is required, it is a form of civic republicanism, combined with an open textured perfectionism. All of these can, I contend, sit happily with liberalism – as post-liberalism – and with democracy, as radical democracy.

The model of citizenship I propose links personal autonomy with political activity. It is the combination of these concepts which is required as components for empowerment and freedom. The outcome of that is an uneasy but healthy tension between the inner recesses of the mind and the outer dimensions of action. It is a combination of citizen and self: a citizen self. It is the citizen self that is able to engage in and be a deep citizen. As I argue it, deep citizenship is the activity of the citizen self acting in a variety of places and spaces. That activity shifts the centre of politics away from the state and so recovers the possibility of politics as an individual participation in a shared and communal activity.

While the actor is individual, the place and focus of the activity is less concerned with the individual than with the shared dimension of the activity. The consequence of that is that the model of deep citizenship is less concerned with rights *per se* than with an ethic of care. That care is towards self, certainly, but it is not merely for the self. As Kant rightly pointed out, self-respect is a requirement of an ethical outlook, but it is also, and equally significantly, guided by a concern for others and the world.

Relating personal autonomy and political concerns might be thought to blur the distinction between what is frequently taken to be social and what is frequently taken to be political. It might also be thought to blur the distinction between what is personal and what is political. In either case the boundaries of politics are extended.

There are two dangers here: the first is that the power of the state becomes extended, and the second is that everything becomes political and that is a recipe for totalitarianism. I propose to avoid the first danger by showing that deep citizenship takes its force from individual action, responsibility and self-awareness and is not an imposition of the state nor a licence to increase the power of the state. I propose to avoid the second danger by arguing for an understanding of politics that is extra-statist. The state rests on a prior conception of politics that it has usurped. The converse of this is that it is perfectly possible to comprehend politics as lying outside of and prior to the domain of the state. There is, I shall argue, a domain of political activity on which the state rests. It is a domain of political activity that falls outside the domain of the state. That condition and that activity can be recovered.

The argument I offer is based in part on the observation that the boundaries between polity and society, between public and private and between state and civil society are blurred and in a state of flux. So much so that I consider it right to regard the public and private not as two distinct domains but as overlapping domains. Sometimes they are identical and sometimes the difference is a matter of emphasis. Civil society has undergone a transformation so profound that it would now be right to regard it as political society.

This ending or blurring of such distinctions is frequently taken to be the conditions for totalitarianism, and arguments of the kind that I propose are generally resisted on those grounds. The fear is I think misplaced. The danger of totalitarianism is real only when respect for individuality, individual autonomy and conscience are absent; when social structure and political structure are identical, and not merely overlapping; when emphases in the interpretation of action are impossible; and when political action has no ethical dimension. The argument I propose avoids these dangers. It is, I shall argue, perfectly possible to understand civil society concerned with economic arrangements as political society.

The possibilities that I sketch lie within the tradition of political thought on which I draw, and are present in embryonic form from its inception. They are, however, possibilities that while realisable have not yet been realised. Inevitably the argument I propose, like so many in political thought, contains a set of *desiderata*. It is, for all that, a set of *desiderata* drawn from a lived tradition and contained within that tradition as a possibility: its actualisation is, of course, a matter of action and not merely a matter of theory. This is not to downplay the role of theory. On the contrary it is significant for it forms part of our self-perceptions and part of our attempts to articulate our position in the world. In political and social life self-perception is not the only measure of how we are, but it is a significant component in that process. This needs some slight explanation. What is real in political terms is, at least partially, what we think is real. Within limits, and there are limits, what we think of as real, what we imagine as that which occurred and what we dream of as part of where we are and where we should be is part of where we are and part of where we intend to go. We cannot make up just any story about ourselves but we can invoke imagination.

One kind of self-perception that we can have is to relate self and political identity in a way that maintains and contains a distinctly reflective and care-full component. The consequence of that is a change of outlook that feeds into a change in political actuality. It is to switch from a generally passive political outlook that is generated by, even required by the state, to an active outlook generated by, even required by, the adoption of a political identity as a significant part of one's mode of life. This extends the bounds of political activity and political action well beyond its normally conceived boundaries. It takes it into dreams and visions, into meaning and poetry without suggesting that such dreams and such imaginations lose contact with actuality.

Politics without vision is no sort of politics at all and to invite others to share a vision is not to suggest it be imposed. What is proposed here falls into the category of an invitation. It is an invitation to conceive or imagine an enhancement of politics in which citizenship is enhanced while avoiding an extension of the boundaries of the state. It is a conception of a form of non-statist politics in which the political dimension of action stems from personal engagement in the world. The distinction between non-statist and statist politics is an important one, for an extension of statist forms of politics, at best, continues that disenchantment with politics which has led to a general disenchantment with the world. At worst, it leads to the interference in everything and with it the end of individuality, autonomy and any ethic, whether that be an ethic of care or an ethic of right and justice.

By contrast to be a deep citizen is to participate both in the operation of one's own life and in some of its parameters; to be conscious of acting in and into a world shared with others; to be conscious that the identity of self and the identity of others is co-related and co-creative; while also opening up the possibility of both engagement in and enchantment with the world.

1

The Death of a Universal

The Commencement of Histories

There is a series of arguments recently developed to the effect that
the underlying premises of Western thought have been based on a
number of mistaken assumptions. Those mistaken assumptions apply
to conventional thought such as traditional liberalism as well as to
its radical opponents, traditional Marxism, for example. The
foundation of this far-reaching claim is that Western thought has
attempted to universalise its own particularity or its own individuality. For example, the claim that liberal democracy is a suitable way
of governance in the West has been extended to the claim that it is
a suitable way of governance throughout the world. Relatedly, the
nation state, a distinctively Western device, has become the standard
by which political communities are adjudged as suitable for
membership in the world community. In all of these cases a particular
aspect or dimension within which political arrangements are comprehended has become the measure by which all political
arrangements are comprehended. To put this in abstract terms the
particular has come to be regarded as the universal. The particular
has come to be regarded as the measure against which other particulars are to be measured. At its best such an outlook represents
loose thinking and at its worst it is little more than a hegemonic device.
    This criticism can and has been levelled at citizenship concepts.
Such concepts universalise and, it is argued, in universalising they
avoid dealing with the real concerns of people. If anything they
actually undercut those concerns by categorising individuals into
classes to which they do not effectively or rightly belong. Later I
will examine the specific claim that citizenship concepts wrongly
universalise. In this chapter I want to show that a significant part
of the crisis in Western thought arises from the death of a universal.
That crisis, however, represents opportunity, an opportunity that
is not only central to the recovery of citizenship but also to the
recovery of politics and the growth of the self as engaged in the world.
    There is a notorious argument to the effect that the engine of
history is driven by great ideological conflicts.[1] The argument goes
on to assert that the great ideological conflicts that have driven it
so far have been between liberalism and communism. The end of

communism, signified most clearly in the fall of the Berlin Wall, has brought about the triumph of liberalism and the end of the conflicts that have driven history. As the engine of history winds down, so history itself comes to an end and liberalism will eventually come to more or less complete world domination.

That argument offered for the end of history is but one instance of a wider species of argument of which the end of philosophy, the end of humanism and the end of humanity are but a few. In some superficial respects there are similarities between all these arguments, but in deeper respects they are fundamentally different. The similarities rest primarily on their focus on Western thought while the differences are in the import and significance of that thought in a period of change. Fukuyama's argument extols the triumph of liberalism, while arguments for the end of philosophy, humanism and man extol the decline of the West. The conflict between these perspectives is a serious one, for the tradition of thought out of which citizenship concepts have arisen is ineluctably Western. If that tradition of thought has come to an end, then citizenship concepts have either come to an end or would require radical transformation to cope with non-Western or post-Western conditions. If, on the other hand, it turns out that Western liberalism is indeed triumphant then Western liberal conceptions of citizenship will also be triumphant. In any event, as liberal conceptions of citizenship are weak, any such triumph would mean the triumph of a weak conception of citizenship. In either case a more radical conception of citizenship such as deep citizenship would have no place.

It is this conclusion that deep citizenship has no place in contemporary political thought that I intend to challenge in this chapter and I will do this in two ways. First, by showing that history rather than being at an end is at its commencement, and second, by showing that the commencement of history in the form of a plurality of histories invokes, among other things, a permission, possibly even a requirement, to comprehend the past in terms of the present. The point of this is to show that citizenship is indeed a Western notion but that it is, for all that, no less meaningful and significant in its own tradition; and also, that radical conceptions and perceptions of citizenship are possible within the confines of a particular tradition of thought while not being confined in some ultimate or final sense to that tradition. Tradition is frequently thought of as constraining and conservative. I shall show that it may also be enabling and radical. The model concept used and utilised here is citizenship, but it may well apply to a whole raft of political concepts. Edmund Burke, in best conservative fashion, described tradition as the embodiment of a pact between the past, the present and the future.[2] I shall argue that it is instead a pact between the present, the past and future and that this difference in perspective produces radical possibilities for the revitalisation and recovery of politics.

The argument to the end of history, as put forward by Fukayama, rests on two different types of observation. The first is a theoretical reading of Hegel filtered through Kojeve, the second is a set of empirical observations about the world. The reading of Hegel sees Hegel as justifying a view of history that moves through several reasonably distinct and discrete stages until it reaches a final culmination. At that point history comes to a conclusion. The empirical observations are that Western values, Western goods and Western ways of life are seen throughout the world. He observes that while it may well be the case that there are aberrations from this, in the long run it is these values that will prevail.

In the Hegelian model the culmination of history varies. Depending on the text it might be the rational state or it might be the ideal ethical order, the *Sittlichkeit* of the *Phenomenology*. In the subsequent Marxist appropriation of the Hegelian perspective on history the outcome was communism. In a twist on this theme, Fukayama attempts to show that the failure of communism shows not the failure of the Hegelian-Marxist model but the failure of communism and the triumph of liberalism. The empirical observations of the actual state of the world are intended to support the theoretical argument, so, as a matter of fact, we find a worldwide adoption of liberal values and liberal aspirations.

While both parts of the argument have some force and have attracted a good deal of attention, both are deeply flawed. While the parts of Fukayama's argument appear to be distinct, as theory on the one hand, and observation on the other, both are closely, even integrally related, and underlying both there is a similar failure. The theoretical part of Fukayama's argument draws on a view of history taken, by Hegel, as World History. The practical part of the argument draws upon observations that take local practices in different parts of the world as either Western practices or variants on Western practices. In bringing all history under a single rubric Hegel ignored vast differences in the experience of different cultures. For example, he took oriental practices as mere precursors to modern Western history, and set aside counter examples as of no consequence. In short he de-historicised that which is historical where it was at variance with his model. Not surprisingly, given that he followed Hegel in this respect, Marx was no less brutal in his interpretation of history. At its starkest Marx describes what he takes as clear stages of history. This started with primitive forms of life which led to ancient and feudal forms of life through to modern or bourgeois modes of production. For Marx, the final victory and the end of history arrives with the end of the capitalist modes of production and the emergence of communism.

For Fukayama, that point has already arrived and is present and evident not in communism, which has collapsed, but in liberal triumphalism. This last argument requires empirical evidence to support it. That evidence is provided, according to Fukayama, in the form of the adoption of liberal values on a worldwide basis.

Each and all of these arguments is flawed in crucial ways. First, they assume that world history is represented in Western history: a practice which in respect of the Westernised interpretation of Eastern cultures has been referred to by Said as 'Orientalism'.[3] Second, it writes out the variety of experiences that people have and interprets them under one rubric. In doing this it eliminates variety in history. Each of these points are subsidiary to the larger claim which rests on an assumption of a universal mankind.

Yet it is just that assumption that is challenged in arguments for the end of humanism and the end of man presented by Nietzsche, Heidegger, Foucault and in a variety of post-modern arguments. Nietzsche had observed that the goal for humanity was still lacking. If this was so then, 'is there not still lacking humanity itself. The goal for humanity is humanity itself'.[4] The failure was manifold but most obviously it is to be found in the conception of humanism itself. In his 'Letter on Humanism' Heidegger traced the roots of the idea of humanism and showed that it was far from a universal notion: it applied instead to particular manners and customs. The consequence of that, if correct, would be to make of the idea of humanism an exclusive rather than an inclusive notion. Humanism originally distinguished between those who adopted certain forms of civility and manners and those who did not, *homo romanus* as opposed to *homo barbaros*.[5] The outcome of this is that humanism tends to be exclusive rather than inclusive; it is particularity masquerading under the guise of universality. Foucault takes the idea of a breakdown in universal categories even further, extending it from the end of humanity to the end of man. The idea of 'man', he claims, is one of recent origin and an idea that is coming to its end.[6]

What each of these attacks on the idea of humanity or the idea of mankind have in common is a concern that the universal, expressed as 'man' or 'human', is not truly universal at all. It is always an expression of a particular conception of what it is to be human or what is to count as 'mankind'. Nietzsche is objecting not to the idea of a common humanity as such but to the fact that there are many competing claims as to what counts as common humanity. In consequence the goal of humanity has not been met. Heidegger is objecting not to the idea of a renewed and revitalised humanism but to the poverty of humanisms that have previously been offered. The objection from Foucault is slightly different in that the self that makes up the humanistic possibility is regarded as a recent and rather weak invention and one with a limited life-span and 'man' is regarded as a construct of temporary convenience.

At its most general what is being objected to is either or both of the ideas that humanity can be expressed in universal terms and that the particularities of life can be subsumed to universal accounts of life. At its most damning the claim is that particular aspects of life have been elevated beyond their particularity into some kind of universality. In such a case the universality is false.

This is just the central problem with the argument that Fukayama offers. It takes one experience – a Western historical experience – and offers that as world history. In this he follows both Hegel and Marx and as he follows them so he makes just the mistakes that they made. As he criticises Marx so he falls prey to the very criticism that he offers. There is no 'liberalism' about which triumphalism is warranted. It is instead the case that there are many liberalisms and they are but one kind of political voice among many in the world. Relatedly it is also the case that Marxism is one voice among many in the world. Marxism attempts to interpret the world in terms that universalise some aspects of the particular experiences of Western societies. To that extent, Marxist, Hegelian and similar outlooks on world history fall prey to the fault of excessive and unwarranted universalisation.

This is not a fault of either Marxism or liberalism as such, it is instead a problem built into the foundations of the Western tradition of thought. It affects Hegel's account of world history and Marxist accounts of world history, for these rest manifestly on attempts to universalise particular experiences. Less obviously, however, it also affects classic liberalism and those models derived from it that continue some central premises from classical liberalism. Premises that cause particular difficulties include: the idea of centred individuals that are the creators of, rather than the products of, society; conceptions that liberalism can be grounded in some absolute or even objective manner; and presumptions that liberalism is a model to be aspired to because of its historical advancement and development towards some historically perceived goal. All of these assumptions rest themselves on a particular religious and theo-logical backdrop, a backdrop that provides the meta-narrative within which the smaller stories of liberalism, Marxism, socialism and all similar grand ideologies make sense.

As a part of that backdrop or meta-narrative we find a variety of claims, such as: 'man' is made in the image of God; history is pro-gressing towards a certain end in which the kingdom of God on earth will be revealed; time has a direction which is linear and history follows that time line in a progressive way. Taken together these assumptions, and they are assumptions for none of them is provable either philosophically or empirically, have provided an almost unchallengeable belief system within which events and other beliefs in the world are justified.

Of course all societies have such belief systems, systems within which their interpretation of the world is given some precedence for them. The difference between most such final beliefs – beliefs that are unchallengeable and generally even beyond discussion – and the basis of Western belief systems is that they rarely carry proselytising force with them, whereas the Western model carries just such an impact. A few examples will suffice to make the general point.

The God in question, while revealed to one people, the Hebraic tribes, came, in Christianity, to be conceived as revealed to them on behalf of the world. The 'man' that is created by that God came to be regarded in early Christianity, and more specifically in Protestantism, as an individual having certain characteristics and certain duties. Those duties involve work, political freedom, freedom of personal conscience and privacy, and those characteristics involve distance from the public realm and the conception of a strong public–private distinction. In consequence, a large part of the public domain was given over to the protection of emerging civil society and the colonialist adventure that went with that. The upshot is a meta-narrative that interpreted its own history as representative of and subsuming all other histories. Other experiences found their way into the Western experience as subservient to it. This dominant hegemonic outlook is expressed with great poignancy in the Roman Catholic Declarations: first, to the effect that non-Christians were barbarians, and second, and more recently, that non-Christians who believed in some other major world religion could be regarded as honorary Christians. In short the alternative belief system, the alterity or otherness, had no legitimacy in its own terms.

This outlook is built into the view that history is a means to some further end, an end to come at some point in the future. Taken to its extreme it interprets all actions and all events as a part of, or aspect of, that final end. Insofar as they are contributors to that end they have little or no meaning of their own. The lives of those that preceded the final end or goal are meaningless in their own terms. If they have a meaning at all it is that they sacrificed their lives to some further historical point.

Some or all of these features find their way into all current forms of liberalism. The consequence of this slightly wider picture of liberalism than is offered by Fukayama is significant. Hegel, Marx and liberalism rest on the same historically eschatological arguments and on a particular conception of history. The failure of that eschatology and that conception of history has brought about the failure of Marxism but it has also brought about the failure of the liberalism that Fukayama espouses and which he mistakenly thinks has triumphed.

The empirical evidence supports this reading. Liberalism has not been welcomed in any significant sense in the Middle East, in China, in the energetic capitalist states of the Pacific rim and in countless other places. Indeed it has been estimated by Caton[7] that the liberal model, however broadly interpreted it might be, has appealed to and been implemented in only a fraction of the world.

The upshot of this is not Western triumphalism but rather its opposite: Western problematisation. Against this backdrop Fukayama's argument cannot succeed but neither can general arguments for some unreconstructed liberalism or for some unre-constructed Marxism succeed for all appear as Western history and experience writ large upon the world. They may appear as universal but this is a mirage for they are little more than particular expressions of vested interests. To pretend that this is anything less than a crisis in politics is to turn away from some major problems in the world – problems that ultimately lead to fragmentation and nihilism. The solution to the difficulty is to find a form of association that recognises the particular while reaching towards the universal.

The arguments that Fukayama put forward, insofar as they are successful at destroying Marxism, are also, unknown or at least unrecognised by him, successful at destroying the liberalism that he takes as the basis for his triumphalism. They are successful in this for all of these models rely on a set of theological assumptions and on an eschatology that collapsed with Nietzsche. The claim that 'God is dead' ushered in the contemporary period and pulled away the assumptions underlying a tradition from its inception. That tradition relied on a particular kind of meta-narrative, an idea that was finally brought to a close by Lyotard.[8]

At its broadest these challenges undercut the idea of the universal contained in the Western tradition of thought, whether it be found in Hobbes, Hegel, Marx, Mill or whoever. Marxism and liberalism, modes of thought that appear to be deeply opposed to each other, share the same fate – insofar as they attempt to legislate for a world beyond their own limits they are little more than ideologies. This seems to indicate the end of the universal as a principal feature of political thought. Yet it was on the attempt to determine the universal that the tradition from Plato through to Christianity developed. The end of that search is, therefore, a significant break with the tradition, so much so that the death of the universal leads to such an excess of its opposite in the form of particularism that it has seemed to some no longer possible to say anything at all beyond the invocation of mere preference. So for MacIntyre, for example, the contemporary world is faced with a mode of morality that is little more than emotivist where emotivism is the view that moral statements express mere individual preferences.[9] Such an outcome seems the logical outcome not of liberal triumphalism but of the end of a single conception of history. The completion of a single conception of history reveals and permits the commencement of multiple conceptions of history. A consequence of that is a variety of divergences in opinions, views and perspectives. The end of history is indeed the end of a single history through which order is mediated and through which hegemony is delivered but it does not leave a complete absence of any and all histories in its wake. On the contrary it reveals a variety of voices hitherto subdued or concealed but which now become part of the commencement of histories. So we may be at the end of history but we are at the commencement of histories and that raises challenges for any broadly inclusive or universal concept.

Whose World is it Anyway?

The history that Kant, Hegel, Marx and Fukayama construct is a particular expression of history. It is Western history with a universal and world perspective of history that lies at its end and its completion. That end has been expressed in a variety of related ways. It is Kantian *Moralität*, the condition that combines virtue and law in a single community existing under conditions of right; Hegel's *Sittlichkeit*, the ideal ethical order; Marx's Communism, the condition that transcends capitalism; or, in Fukayama's reading, it is liberalism. In any or either of these cases it is the order so expressed that turns out to be the universal standard against which the rest of the world is judged and against which the activities and projects within it succeed or fail.

All such conceptions of the world, however they might be expressed, assume that there is but a single world in which we live. To some extent this is clearly correct, for while we live in many overlapping 'worlds' there is a sense in which, however problematic and fuzzy the concept might be, we live in only one World. But this conception raises a difficulty for, while we live in only one World, that in itself raises the question as to whose world is it anyway? The traditional answer has been top-down and hegemonic, and a European hegemony at that. Fukayama's triumphalism is but one aspect of a wider phenomenon for, until recently, European history has been regarded as world history. Kant, Hegel, Marx and latterly Fukayama have all taken particular characteristics of European history and universalised them.[10]

When the particular becomes universalised it inverts itself and turns into ideology. As it inverts itself that which is merely contingent appears as necessary. The world, Marx said when criticising capitalism, is seen upside down as in a *camera obscura*.[11] Yet even as he was saying this, and even as he was inverting the inversion of the world, he was simultaneously making the particular Western passage from feudal to capitalist economic conditions the basis of world history. As he did this so he was committing the very error that he was scorning. It is this failure that is at the basis of the collapse of Marxism, but it is a failure not of Marxism alone but simultaneously of numerous components within the Western tradition of thought.

In consequence this generalised critique of Marx holds equally of liberalism. Fukayama's argument that the end of history will ultimately result in the triumph of liberalism lays bare the intimate, even ineradicable, basis of the relation between Hegel, Marx and liberalism. That there is such a close relation is scarcely surprising, for looked at from an appropriately distant perspective, both have arisen from the same conditions and from the same tradition of thought. In consequence both have interpreted the world in broadly similar terms. This is not to say that there are not substantial differences between them, but they are differences within a framework of viewing the world in a broadly similar way. Indeed the fact that there can be a long-running and meaningful debate between Marxist and liberal modes of thought shows not their differences but their similarities.[12]

This observation may seem surprising in an age that has taken Marxism and liberalism as radically opposing ideas. Yet it ought not to be surprising for both are drawn from the same broad tradition and both rely on similar premises, albeit worked out in different ways. The consequence of that is that their fate is inextricably tied together. Of course Marxism, as a systematic ideology, is by common consent, dead. But, given the shared premises, liberalism, or at least that part of it that takes European history and purely European characteristics as universal, and that part of it that takes civil society as unpolitical, is equally dead. Both Marxism and liberalism are, or at least until recently have been, theories making universal claims; claims not just about history, but also about the beings in history. They have treated such beings as either relatively passive and shaped by history or relatively active, significant movers in the shaping of history. This observation requires, perhaps, some comment.

At its broadest the Western tradition of thought has developed from a number of sources occasionally consonant yet often in tension. From its Hellenistic origins it takes, in broad terms, the idea of reality as provided by that which is beyond experience. From its Hebraic-Christian roots it takes an apocalyptic tradition of thought which sees the end of history expressed in messianic terms or in terms of some *parousia*, some account of the kingdom of God on Earth. This unique confluence of different strands of thought resulted in an account of history that universalised itself and wrote its particular experience as either world history or as representative of world history. At its most blatant it finds itself expressed in the idea of the Christian empire and/or the Protestant ethic and its drive towards the domination of the world. In secular form it is found, on the one hand, in the perspective that some kind of communism is the end point of world history or, on the other hand, in the perspective expressed by, among others, Fukayama, that liberalism is the end of history.

The claim that the end of history is to be found in communism has failed and obviously so. But the failure is less a consequence of overwhelming intellectual arguments than a failure of the underlying conditions on which the perspective rested. In particular the meta-narrative on which the tradition that spawned a view that there is an end to history has collapsed. That general collapse has led to a more particular collapse of various pictures of the end of history. So the view that communism is at the end of history has collapsed, not as a consequence of arguments against communism but as a consequence of the collapse of the meta-narrative structure on which such an account rested. Once that collapse occurs the necessity apparently contained in the tradition also collapses and the reality of its contingency emerges. The collapse of that meta-narrative is not to be found with Marx, for that theory is secularised eschatology; it is more properly to be placed with Nietzsche, for it is at that point, more than in Marx, that the very foundations of Western thought were placed into question. The claim that 'God is dead' destroyed the Christian meta-narrative, but it destroyed also the Marxist eschatology and the Marxist theory of history. The consequence of that collapse is not limited to a failure of communism as some end point of history; it extends also to any other account of the end of history. It is the idea that there is a progression of which the end of history is the consequence that collapses. A perspective that the end of history is to be found in some kind of liberal triumphalism is as vulnerable to the collapse of the meta-narrative as some conception that the end of history is to be found in some other *eschates*, communism, for example. A consequence of this is that the end of the historical certainties that led to the decline of communism are equivalent to the decline of certainties that perceived liberalism as ultimately dominant.

The end of the supremacy of either or both of these views is not merely a pragmatic occurrence that has some limited value for some aspects of Western thought. It has implications of an even wider sort, primarily, and possibly even dangerously, for the destruction of any form of universalism. Again the Platonic and Christian sources developed, or allowed to be developed, the idea that there is one mode of life that ought to be adopted. Classically that was expressed as the good, as in Plato, or the Holy Roman Empire, the Christian Empire and the colonial hegemony of nationalistic and imperialistic Europe. More latterly it is expressed as perfectionism: the idea that there is a perfect order to be obtained. This is sometimes expressed as the non-liberal view that the good is prior to the right. One kind of liberal response to this has been to take liberal claims in a pragmatic rather than a universalistic sense.

A clear example of the pragmatic liberal response can be found in Rorty's claim that in our society liberalism is part of the final discourse of a society. It is just the way 'we do things',[13] and liberalism, he seems to think, will turn out to be the last intellectual revolution needed. Such a conclusion is far from easy to justify. To claim that some one thing is the last instance of that sort of thing seems little more than a pragmatic example of that mode of apocalyptic-eschatological thought which spawned old liberalism and old Marxism alike.

The incredulity towards meta-narratives[14] that has become definitive of post-modernity might seem to bring the enterprise of constructing a satisfactory model of citizenship to a close. First, citizenship is a distinctively Western notion; second, it lies clearly within that framework of thought that falls broadly under the *aegis* of the collapsed meta-narrative; and third, as I shall argue, it universalises in an age that increasingly seeks particularities. It might appear that these objections would be enough to undercut the notion of citizenship completely. That they are not, and that they can be responded to in an adequate way, is a principal thesis of this book. One part of that response is to observe that of any political concept some origin is required. But that origin is not necessarily determinative of the final outcome. It might, like Wittgenstein's ladder, be something up which one climbs in order to throw it away when the journey has been completed.

Starting Somewhere

To break from the meta-narratives that spawned liberalism and Marxism alike, while retaining important and significant aspects of the political tradition, requires the redefinition, reconstrual and reconstruction of political activity. The reconstruction of the political that is involved in such an activity carries with it the reconstruction of citizenship and the re-orienting of conceptions of the self. I will later argue that such a re-orientation includes the conception of the citizen self. The concept of the citizen self contains deliberate ambivalences within it and necessarily lacks either complete unity or unification. The force of the internal plurality of the concept of the citizen self will become clearer later. The reconstruction of the political also requires a re-conceptualisation of history, for the collapse of the meta-narrative destroys a major dimension through which order in history has been perceived and maintained. The collapse of a major platform through which order in history has been maintained releases a variety of competing voices, voices that have hitherto been silenced or ignored. Hearkening to those voices is a significant part of political revitalisation and including those voices in citizenship concepts is a vital part of the revitalisation of those notions.

The real end of history is the end of a single account of history and the commencement of a variety of histories. Within that variety of histories there is a variety of voices each telling separate narratives. Within those narratives significance is more attached to the local than to the meta-narrative. A consequence of that is that there is no common starting point. If there is no common starting point there is no single concept that can serve as a foundation for subsequent discussion. This is a real problem that is thrown up by contemporary circumstances. Taken to its extreme it leads either to the nihilism of silence or to the nihilism of radical particularism.

In consequence it is necessary that there be starting points. In the case of citizenship concepts the starting points must reside in Western society and its predecessors: not because that is some final arbiter of what counts as citizenship, but because that is the origin of those concepts and because any conversation has to start somewhere.

The conversation that is citizenship contains such a marked degree of Western components that its examination does have to start with the Western tradition. There is no social or cultural *tabula rasa* on which to write a new book, and starting points do determine end points 'to some extent'. The qualifier 'to some extent' is critical, and is the point at which the approach here departs from the eschatological tradition while still retaining much of its valuable imagery. The eschatological tradition, within which theological imagery and political argument from Marx to the liberal triumphalism of Fukayama are contained, fixed beginnings and ends. They contain what theologians refer to as first and last days.

The apocalyptic-eschatological tradition is found in a variety of theologically inspired sources from Daniel to the revelations of John and beyond. It is also found in a variety of modified and secularised forms in Kant, Hegel, Marx and liberal triumphalism. Each of these contain images of first and last days. Generally such models contain the detail of the last days in the first days. They are deterministic. This determinism has a specific content about the end of history or even, as in models of predestination, specific models about the final disposal of the end of a particular life.

The model offered here differs from the traditional account in several ways. Most significantly there is fluidity in the outcome arising from a particular beginning. While the range of possible world end points is contained in the beginning, any *particular* end point is not. This distinction between the model of the first and last days contained in the apocalyptic-eschatological tradition and developed in a variety of forms in Western thought and the position proposed here is significant. The model that I propose implies that the first days are determinative only of the general kinds of problems and the general kinds of solutions offered by a tradition. It does not assume that the specific detail of what is contained at the end is contained in the model laid down at the outset. The difference is important and significant. Concepts, ideas, practices and institutions embed outlooks and orientations but they do not completely fix the content, for the specificity that attaches to the orientations and outlooks is open textured.

This open texturedness is not trivial – on the contrary it is central in its most general terms to a life of personal growth and autonomous development. More particularly it is required for the reconstruction of citizenship, the recovery of politics and the project of radical democracy. These latter aims are part of a programme of widespread democratisation. Democratisation, in this sense, is active participation in a significant and relatively autonomous way in shared aspects of the world. To be involved in one's own life instead of being disengaged from it, to be an actor rather than an unwilling or distanced spectator, is an ideal contained deep in Western thought but one that is far from realised. To aim at its realisation necessarily involves some perfectionism; but it does not follow that any particular content or any particular and restrictive programme need be prescribed merely by that perfectionism.

This is a significant change from traditional perfectionist conceptions. The weakness of traditional perfectionisms, from at least Plato onwards, has been to link goals and content. Thus one repeatedly comes across the formula that the good life requires just *this* or just *that* sort of social and political order... the blanks can be filled in as appropriate. In the eschatologically underpinned models, whether Marxist, socialist or liberal, the linkage between the first and last days was mistakenly thought to be necessary. It is on this basis that socialism, communism and/or liberalism could be prescribed. Relatedly, and more widely, the linkage between the good life and a particular or specific order was also, and mistakenly, thought to be necessary.

It is a mistake for it is not necessary that the good life contain any particular content. On the contrary there is every reason to think that there are a variety of ways in which human flourishing might be maximised and human suffering might be minimised. *Summum bonum* is less *the summum bonum* than *a summum bonum*. This re-conceptualisation of what counts as a good for humankind is significant for it shifts the initial conceptualisation of what counts as good from a single prescription to a number of possible pre-scriptions. Perfectionism moves from being closed to becoming open textured.

There are interesting and quite radical consequences to the shift proposed here. If perfectionism is open textured, so the appropriate and related social and political arrangements are open textured. Indeed it is required that they be so. It is also required that the open texturedness is limited and not infinite. To say that there are open possibilities is not to say that *any* possibility is open and that any possibility is morally permissible. Many social and political arrangements match the requirement for leading a life that is significantly one's own while also being in the company of others; but not all and any social and political arrangements meet that requirement. Open texturedness does not license for instance, barbarism, fascism, Nazism and a thousand other cruel and destructive forms of political life that have either been found or that are yet to be found. It is clear that enough of the aspects of the actual world in which we find ourselves do not meet the requirements of permitting and encouraging a mode of life that is one's own. If they fail in that task so they fail in the broader enterprise of permitting or encouraging the development of significant concepts of citizenship.

What can be said about social and political arrangements in the wider sense, the general structures, institutions and practices, can be said about the actions of individuals as *engagè* in the world. And when they are so engaged they are, I shall argue, citizens. When they are more than passingly engaged, conscious, and careful of that engagement and willing to extend its range into care for self, others and the world, they are also, I shall argue, engaged with the world as deep citizens.

To be engaged in the world as a deep citizen is to be engaged with others and with the world. But it is not, as with perfectionisms of old, to prescribe the content or mode of expression of those relations. Nor is it, as with the apocalyptic-eschatological tradition, to specify any particular content to any particular last days. An example drawn from a pragmatic yet phenomenological reading of religion is illustrative. William James[15] argued that religious experience is a valuable *particular* experience that is universally experienced but in different ways in different cultures. That there is a phenomenon that is universally experienced does not of itself justify universal or normative claims about either the content of that experience, the forms of life that are associated with it, or any particular good, or religion. The particular does not legislate the universal and the universal does not legislate the particular but this does not imply that they are completely and always torn asunder. Of course they do, in an open life, co-exist in tension. It is that tension that is required for openness, change, and ultimately for radical democracy.

It is that tension, a tension that manifests itself in a variety of ways, that is required also for deep citizenship. Put in positive terms it is possible to take engagement in life with others in a world in which others live as a universal good, but such a claim does not prescribe the content or expression of particular activities. Put in negative terms, to embrace an open-ended and open-textured view of political activity does not license just any activity or just any attitude. To accept particularity as valuable does not of itself imply that all particularities are to be accepted as valuable. On the contrary some particular forms of life, some particular practices, institutions, attitudes and habits, for example, torture, brutalisation, excessive and wanton restrictions on freedom, may be condemned. They can be condemned because the particular is never found in entirely pure form: the universal is always there as part of the tension that makes the particular possible: an excess of particularism leads to selfishness, sectarianism and sectionalism, characteristics that are personally implosive rather than personally expansive.

The tensions between the universal and the particular are ineliminable, and are potentially harmful; but they are also potentially helpful. Of course some concepts and models of thought veer more one way than another. Some concepts and models of thought seek, often unwittingly, to eliminate one at the expense of the other. So it is with citizenship. Classic, modern and contemporary models of citizenship have tended to be limited in focus and universalistic in their foundations and prescriptions. This is their weakness. They apply widely, and often falsely, while also eliminating significant difference. They are, in consequence, of limited effect in the living of real people: they are shallow. Deep citizenship, as I construe it, is a radical alternative to shallow citizenship. This radical alternative requires accepting the uneasiness between the universal and the particular without surrendering to either.

To surrender to universalism, as with shallow citizenship, would be to categorise everyone or some aspect of everyone under a single head. That move is the stuff of a bygone, imperialistic and hegemonic age. On some extreme accounts all universalistic claims should, therefore, be abandoned. I will argue that universalism *per se* is not a problem. The problem lies more with almost all hitherto existing forms of universalism in that they make *a priori* prescriptions. They legislate what people's lives and living ought to be on the basis of preconceived ideas, ideas that bear little or no relation to actual lives and actual living. But it does not follow from this that the experience of successful living cannot lead to a discovery of what goes into successful living. A possible *a posteriori* universalism is an entirely open and healthy approach to discovering what might make the framework of successful living. By contrast *a priori* assumptions to that end lie somewhere between the arrogant and the imperialistic.

Deep citizenship, as that model is worked through here, expresses a form of being that permits the reaching towards an *a posteriori* universality. The universalism is discovered in the course of actual living and actual experience rather than being an imposition on lives and living. In arising out of actual living deep citizenship pays attention to difference and alterity instead of existing merely as an attachment to a mode of being that imposes universality and inhibits difference.

The model of citizenship that I develop here, deep citizenship, takes living itself to be political, in the sense that in self, other and world engagement it connects with shared being. In consequence deep citizenship belongs at the intersection of that part of the radical democratic project that holds that such a project is well furthered by a recovery of the political. Radical democracy fuses that individuality which is found in the best of post-liberalism with a serious conception of sociality found in the best of post-Marxism. Radical democracy moves beyond both in setting an agenda for the new millennium. That agenda includes the view that while we work in and with traditions there are moments of discontinuity and opportunities for effecting significant changes. The past is sedimented in the present, but what we do at times of rupture and discontinuity becomes part of the sedimentation of the far future and that sedimentation is largely ours to make, not, perhaps, entirely as we please but to make within limits as we please. In short we can, even while being required to work within some givens, make a difference to the future.

Because there is no social, political or cultural *tabula rasa*, I start with an analysis of the different types of citizenship that have been found since the inception of that concept and show that, even at its most penetrating and noblest, citizenship, hitherto, has been limited in crucial ways. Given some significant changes in the relation between civil society and state, and between public and private, that limitation is no longer appropriate to the challenge of democratising diverse elements of contemporary life.

That democratisation is contained within some aspects and usages of the language of liberalism and in its predecessors, but such usages also contain a deep contradiction. On the face of it liberalism demands individual responsibility and individual empowerment as part of its individualistic programme, yet at the same time, by refusing to politicise society, it inhibits that very empowerment.

In the context of the Western political tradition at least, one starting point for that empowerment is to be found in the idea of radical democracy. This is the taking of the unfinished business of democracy as it is found in Ancient Greece, and even earlier in the mytho-poesis of Mesopotamia, and extending it to all members of civil society. In turn that requires, as it expresses itself four millennia later in the twenty-first century, the transformation of civil society into a newly reconstructed political society.

This is a switch or transformation contained in embryonic form in the roots of the tradition. It is also a significant switch that has already taken place. Civil society is effectively a political place. Yet for all that there is a tendency both in theory and in practice to cling to the fiction that there is a clear distinction between state and civil society or that there is a clear distinction between the public and the private. I shall argue that such distinctions do not hold in anything other than fictitious ways.

Rousseau took it that the purpose of the Social Contract was to 'share in the operation of one's own life'. That ideal is not yet redundant and has yet to be realised in any significant way. It is contained in a number of sources of which Rousseau is but one. Perhaps its most noble expression is contained in William of Moerbecke's conception of *polistheuma* and in Dante's *politizare*. In either case the underlying idea is that to live a fully engaged life is to live politically. To be human is to be engaged not in some other-worldly enterprise but to be engaged in this worldly enterprise: as I construe it this is the foundation of deep citizenship. In a significant sense to be is to be political.

A community in constructing itself writes and rewrites its history not in an objective way but in an imaginary, albeit limited, way. Behind that claim lie a variety of theoretical justifications. I will mention just a few. First, (the allegedly and mistakenly regarded conservative) Michael Oakeshott in his detailed examination of what counts as a history,[16] sets objective accounts of history aside in favour of an account of history that draws on the historian rather than on some apparent model of what allegedly and objectively took place. In sum we cannot know the past 'as such' – what we know is what we imagine to be the case about the past. This imagination is an aspect of the present and not an objective feature of the past. Second, Cornelius Castoriadis[17] invokes the idea of the social imaginary to account for the manner and way in which communities come to regard themselves as communities. Third, as Benedict Anderson points out,[18] communities construct an imaginary past which legitimates its present and which binds it in its present form.

Relations between people and between their perceptions of each other rest on a complex set of intentions, dispositions and general orientations that they share. A community is a set of shared relations understood internally more than it is a set of objective behaviours. In a significant sense it resides in the imaginations of the members of that community. In building up a shared identity a community comes to have a set of shared intentions and dispositions about its past, its general account of its origins, of its place in the cosmos, of paradigmatic figures and personages that come to represent significant perceptions of its history and events that mark significant moments in its shared memory. It matters not whether such personages or such events actually existed or took place; what is of concern is that the people involved take it that they did and orient themselves accordingly.

This does not imply that the past did not exist. It does imply, however, that the past does not exist for us in some objective sense: it exists rather as imagination, poetry and myth that feeds into our conceptions of the present. At its deepest it occurs and presents itself to us as that part of our social imaginary that recalls, often in mytho-poetic form, that which a society comes to regard as its beginnings.

This imaginary historical foundation I shall call the social originary. Any social originary is of course someone's social originary. To that extent it is partial, particularistic and limited. This is unavoidable. There has to be some actual starting point and a starting point that erred towards the pure universal would empty itself of content and meaning. The avoidance of the twin traps of excessive universality or excessive particularity requires a starting point that straddles both these facets.

The concept of citizenship and the political tradition that goes with that is rooted in particular accounts of the past. Those accounts are specifically Western, yet they have occupied an aspect of the meta-narrative on which the structure of order has been based. As those accounts have collapsed or been challenged so the traditional structure of order has been challenged, and new orders and new demands emerge.

Citizenship concepts and the associated conceptions of politics are a part of a particular history that was writ large as universal history. In consequence those concepts were universalised. In a world of competing voices, competing histories and competing world perceptions their weakness is that they are unjustified, universalising concepts.

In the next chapter I begin with an account of our social imaginary that recalls the very beginnings of the Western mode of thought. It is our social originary almost as far as we can account for it. Perhaps it is real and recalls an understanding from long ago. Perhaps it is a figment of the imagination of the translator who, lost in the present, can interpret the past only in the terms now available. It matters not, for in either case it forms part of the imagination of where we are now, and in either case it invokes the radical possibilities that result from the breakdown of a single model of history.

The end of a single history is the commencement, in a number of senses, of a variety of histories. First, it brings the single meta-narrative to an end, in that sense it is the end of a single history. A model of world history is always someone's single perspective on the world. Second, the collapse of a single account of history opens up a variety of competing historical possibilities. Where communities have had their unique history subverted to Western history a variety of relatively autonomous histories emerge. Third, 'the activity of being an historian'[19] is not the uncovering of some 'objective' past. The past does not exist for us in that sense; it exists, rather, as a variety of imaginings in those who invoke it. There are, therefore, many possible histories of the same people and many possible histories of the world. The end of history brings about the commencement of histories – a multitude of voices seeking to be heard and which are the foundation not of the once but of the future politics. It is this challenge which traditional conceptions of citizenship fail to meet and to which the concept of deep citizenship is addressed.

2

Of Myths, Mirrors and Origins

Citizenship offers the opportunity to participate in one's own life and in the creation and re-creation of the conditions within which that life is acted out. It is an idea with both promise and failure, the latter sometimes being regarded as so complete that instead of being a politically emancipatory device citizenship can come to be a device that politically neuters entire populations. A clear example of a non-political dimension to citizenship occurs when it is treated as a device of mere status.

As mere status citizenship is a device that excludes anything other than a minimal political involvement by most people. It may be so successful in this exclusion that it is part of a generalised and almost invisible hegemony.

In its universalising sense citizenship has attempted to relate distinct people together by subsuming individuals, no matter what their real and lived distinctions might be, as members of a single category. This may have some merit and some advantage in homogeneous social arrangement but in the kind of heterogeneous and egalitarian arrangement now found it is fraught with problems. Such problems have been well represented in, for example, those feminist arguments that citizenship ignores the political significance of gender and is endemically and ineradicably masculine and patriarchal. Similar arguments can be raised from other directions, so that, for instance, it can be said that citizenship ignores the political effects of race, ethnicity, religion and a host of other categories which people take as crucial to their life.[1] If this is so then citizenship, while ostensibly universalising, misses some important points about the particular and important dimensions of real lives.

These objections are significant. But their significance would be lessened if they were merely objections to the practice of citizenship as it is currently found. I do not think this is the case. There are many problems with the way in which citizenship has been developed and utilised in present as well as in previous times. Some of those problems have been specific to particular times but some of those problems reach beyond particular times into the foundations of the concept of citizenship.

26

In the next two chapters I will deal with these concerns. Citizenship offers much as ideal and much as promise but before it can be established just how much ideal and promise can be met it is necessary to see just how deep the problems in the concept run; I will argue that this is very deep indeed. The correction of these problems will require a re-conceptualisation of citizenship that itself runs very deep but which is not so far from the existing political and social situation as to be unattainable.

In the next chapter I will argue that to have the status of a citizen and to be an active citizen are distinctions which, while having a long pedigree and being the subject of much debate and acrimony, are no longer, if they ever were, significant. For the moment I want to turn to the way citizenship has turned up in some of the most basic accounts of the social originary that placed Western society on the path it subsequently followed. Citizenship as currently conceived differs little from its earliest imaginings.[2]

In the first part of this chapter I will show that the problems in the notion of citizenship are not incidental but are built into the concept right from its foundation. Those problems are seriously exacerbated by a complete collapse of the mythical glue which kept the components together. In the second part I will show that the problem of inappropriate universalisation is no mere happenstance, but is a problem arising both from the history of the citizenship concepts and from the mechanism of universalisation itself. In the third part I will show the inherent tendency of citizenship concepts to be removed from the concerns of people.

In Search of Roots

Any social institution draws on a narrative structure within which it becomes sensible and meaningful to its participants. That narrative structure contains both immediate and general accounts. The widest and most general account is the meta-narrative, the story within which basic questions and outlooks are contained and which shapes and gives meaning to particular narratives, whether that be in the form of the history of a people or a country, or in the biography of an individual person.

Well known meta-narratives that have played an important part in Western life are, among others: the Hebraic-Christian account of the formation and conclusion of the world; a related apocalyptic-eschatological account or some semi-secular equivalent as in Kant or Hegel; some entirely secular equivalent as in Marxism, Marxism-Leninism; or liberal triumphalism *qua* Fukayama. The collapse of the meta-narrative as a general idea and a general supporting structure for modes of life has come to place those structures in jeopardy, for what seems necessary within the structure of the meta-narrative comes to seem merely contingent when the meta-narrative is withdrawn.

One consequence of that shift is to make what might appear to be minor events and perceptions of the past more, not less, significant. When the course of history and/or the structures and relations within history are regarded as determined, minor, and sometimes even major, events seem of little consequence in the longer run. By contrast, when the course of history and relations within history are regarded as undetermined what might seem like minor events appear as significant. It might be thought that one consequence of the shift from a history perceived in terms of necessity to a history perceived in terms of contingency is to make all events seem of equal importance. This would be a mistake, for paradoxically it is more the case that in an age after history it is the earliest events that are the most significant and the more recent events, even if they seem of greater magnitude, that are the more minor.

The paradox is easy to comprehend. The starting events lay down or sediment practices, beliefs, structures, languages and linguistic practices, world outlooks and perspectives in a way that later events do not. It is the starting events that determine the general possible outlines of the later world and later events occur within that shape. Whoever began the cultural ripple had a far greater effect than anyone far from the starting point.

That initial starting point is part of the social imaginary, more specifically it is that part of the social imaginary which is bound up with what I will call the social originary. I define the social originary as that part of the social imaginary which images its roots and foundations. The social originary is a kind of cultural mirror in that it provides an image of where we are now, expressed in images and terms that are distinct from immediate concerns. At its starkest the social originary is what might have been regarded as one or more of the founding components of the meta-narrative. To take one influential example: the account of the expulsion from paradise, the Fall, which resulted from the disobedience by Adam and Eve of the prime interdiction not to eat from the fruit of the tree of knowledge, became the foundation of Paulian and Augustinian accounts of history, will and freedom. Transformed it became definitive of humanism in Dante, transformed again it became the foundation of liberal individualism and transformed in alternative manner it became the foundation of the account of history underlying Marxism and Fukayama's liberal triumphalism. The end of history, whether it be in the version given by Hegel, Marx or Fukayama could be conceived only against a conceptual background, principal components of which were provided in the idea of the Fall and the narrative developed from that.

In such cases the world has been affected in significant and varying ways by an initial story or stories whose truth value ranges from the indeterminable to the false and which latterly has come to be, as all such accounts have come to be, regarded with incredulity. Once it is seen as inappropriate to attach a truth value to such narratives they come to be seen as determinative of the way in which a culture has learnt to understand and interpret itself. The myth is determinative of the actuality of events, attitudes and self-under-standings. Its value lies not in its claimed literality, but in the framework it has provided for a culture to interpret and continu-ously reinterpret itself.

History examined in this way contains no strong distinction between some claimed objective history and some reconstructed or newly imagined history. The social originary is not concerned with what really happened in the past as such, or with what people really did or what people really said. These do affect the social originary but they are not its prime concern. Similarly, attempts to recover some meaning or event or understanding from the past might inform readings of the social originary but they do not determine it.

The imagery of the social originary is presented most starkly in mythical or poetic-mythical form, but it is by no means confined to that form. It might also contain what appear to be logical, philo-sophical, theological, ethical, social, political or historical terms and ideas. Often such images, ideas and perspectives will be mixed together: they will never completely be separated. A philosophical or scientific account of foundations will always contain social and theological components and a sociological account always has theology, philosophy and myth embedded in it.

The clearest and most obvious accounts of origins draw on precursors that are found in even more ancient myths, fragments of which, while influential, would have been absorbed in even earlier adoptions of even prior mythical origins. That process of adoption and absorption is usually so complete that its origins are forgotten. There are numerous examples. The story of the flood as it appears in the Old Testament is pre-empted in earlier Mesopotamian myths. Some of those components are now available in fragmentary form and provide a basis for readings of where we now are: we can reconstruct, in part at least, some of the earliest dimensions of the social originary of what has come to be thought of as 'Western society'.

It might seem from this that the social originary is just an invention. In a way it is, for it is informed by and cannot escape the inventions of the past. To that extent it is a cumulative invention. But it is not a pure or haphazard invention for it is fed by events and imaginings and fragments of events and fragments of imaginings from the past. A society cannot have just *any* social originary and it cannot make up just *any* tale about itself. That would be a mere revisionism of the kind sometimes adopted in tyrannies. In such cases reality is altered in considerable ways but it does seem that such enterprises frequently founder when the revision oversteps what is possible.[3] There are many conceivable pasts but not all such pasts are meaningful, significant or sustainable.

When we look at that part of the social originary which exhibits political beginnings we see something recognisable but distant. It is recognisable partly because the events behind it fed into our culture and our practices, but it is recognisable also because that is the way we read it and the way that we are, to some extent, conditioned to read it. The relation between that part of the social imaginary that is concerned with present expressions and the social originary is one of interrelationship. The past feeds the present but the present also feeds and informs the past.[4]

That part of the social originary which contains citizenship concepts is usually thought of as starting in Ancient Greece. As an idea and a concept, if not a word, this is so and I will look at the Greek experience shortly. I want, however, to start with a story, or at least a myth that goes back well before the normal accounts of the origin of citizenship but which provides the foundation for an idea that came to be incorporated into the idea of citizenship. The myth is traced to the Ancient Mesopotamian pantheon: the assembly of gods.

The assembly, so the myth has it, meets to debate, to make judgments and to determine the execution of its judgments. Sometimes the debate and judgments concern the gods only, sometimes they concern actions the gods take against mankind. Sometimes the action in that godly polity is agonistic, as when the gods act for themselves in the assembly, when they speak for their own interests and their own issues. Sometimes, however, the action of the gods is representative, as when the gods act on behalf of others, usually humans. With humans they seem to have a mixed relationship. Sometimes they think well of humans, but frequently they think ill of them. The equality between the gods of the pantheon is notable but it is not complete. There is an apparent equality of voice in the assembly but for all that some gods are clearly higher in rank than others.

A clear example that contains all these features is found in the poem *Lament for Ur*. The assembly of gods meets to discuss the future of the city of Ur. Prior to the formal business they solemnly agree to abide by the decisions of the assembly. The future of the city is placed in the hands of the assembly and the goddess of Ur, Ningal, pleads for its continuing survival. When it is proposed to destroy the city of Ur and all the men in it Ningal, the goddess who is the protector of Ur, beseeches the assembly to spare the city and its inhabitants.

'May my city not be destroyed!'
    I said indeed to them.
'May Ur not be destroyed!' I said indeed to them.
'And may its people not be killed!'
    I said indeed to them.
But An never bent towards those words,
and Enlil never with an, 'It is pleasing, so be it!'
    did soothe my heart.[5]

She appeals in particular to the head of the assembly, but to no effect.

There is no revoking a verdict,
a decree of the assembly,
a command of An and Enlil
is not known ever to have been changed.[6]

The outcome is that the city is destroyed, along with its inhabitants.

The truth or falsity of the myth is of less significance than its components and its general effect as a symbolic part of the social originary. The pantheon is the earliest description available to us of a polity in miniature. The gods are the effective citizens in that polity.

The pantheon in its hierarchical structure and then in its collective gatherings, in assembly, contains all the components that were to be found in the human *polis* and contains them in the same way as the human *polis* developed in Greece more than a millennia and a half later. Whether one takes it that the gods direct the human, the ancient model, or whether one takes it that gods are a projection of the humans, the contemporary model, is immaterial.

Consequently the truth or falsity of this myth, and its correct or incorrect translation across almost five millennia, is less important than its structural significance. It contains within it all the components of the polity that found its way into Ancient Greece from the rise of the *polis* after about 750 BC and it contains within it all the components that make up politics as we understand that today.

The *polis* contains a space or domain wherein the action takes place and the form of that action is broadly agonistic. The development of the notion of the *agon* arises from Greek drama. It is that point in the play when the principal contestants enter the stage and engage in verbal confrontation. The confrontation is important as is the verbal nature of it. Speech, appearance, presentation and argument are crucial to the *agon*, but so also is domain. The domain or place of the action is centre stage.

The myth of the pantheon is the first occasion in which there is an assembly of actors, a domain of interaction, a debate between gods acting on their own behalf and of gods acting on behalf of others, making a case for and representing the interests of the cities and the people they protected. The decision of the pantheon is final and its decisions are handed over to an executor. There is even the foundation of a basic division between legislature and executive to be found here. That such a model can be found more than four millennia ago indicates the depth of this conception of government.

As the gods, so the humans. The pantheon of Ancient Greece contained distinction, division and debate, and, as with the Mesopotamian pantheon, it also contained hierarchy. In both cases the model of the pantheon expresses in mytho-poetic form the perceived model of human life. If the gods could govern themselves in such a way, so could humans.

The tradition that generated politics from the pantheon also generated a critique of the pantheon. The foundation of the *polis* as a form of right order also generated the possibilities of a break with that order. One of the most significant turning points is found in Book II of Plato's *Republic* when he introduced the word 'theology' into the world as the idea that one might talk in a critical manner of the gods. The introduction of that idea contained the critical tradition that finally emerged in Nietzsche's claim that God was dead and with it the gradual emergence of an attitude of 'incredulity towards meta-narratives'.[7]

Yet that incredulity is neither simple, automatic nor without consequence. Politics is frequently regarded as being in permanent tension with theology. There are three prime reasons for that tension. First, it is a consequence of the critical attitude towards the gods out of which the political tradition emerged. Second, it is a consequence of worldly nature of politics as opposed to the unworldly nature of theology. Third, the narrative that began the political tradition and the narrative that provided the later part of the theological tradition have frequently emerged in opposition. The opposition frequently emerges as a contest as to which course of action has the greater claim, the political or public or some higher law.

When, for instance, to take an early, well-known, even paradigmatic example, Antigone breaks the law it is not because she does not recognise it as a law but because she challenges its limitations. In response to Creon she clearly admits knowledge of its public nature. For all that she considers it to be limited in effect. This, for her, justifies the claim that disobedience to the public law is permitted for,

It wasn't Zeus, not in the least,
who made this proclamation – not to me.
Nor did that Justice, dwelling with the gods
beneath the earth, ordain such laws for men.
Nor did I think your edict had such force
that you, a mere mortal, could override the gods.[8]

The structure and the challenge itself is significant. The structure permits a challenge to the public dimension on grounds that are wider than those normally admitted. Antigone ultimately dies for the sake of the larger concerns, but in so doing she draws out some tensions that permit what I will later come to characterise as *deep citizenship*.

These myths show, among other things, the agonistic and direct foundation of politics. They show the connection of politics to theology and show how the originary of politics is in conflict with the originary of the myth of the Fall. There is a congruence of meta-narratives in some respects and an incongruence in others. The social and political originary that contained the vital component of Western thought and politics contained a series of irresolvable tensions in it. Those tensions have been held together in varying ways, primarily under the Christian apocalyptic–eschatological meta-narrative. The end of that meta-narrative has released the tensions contained within the tradition and brought that which appeared a necessity in history to the forefront as mere contingency.

There are a number of consequences that follow. A few are, one, the tensions are revealed as fractures; two, the fractures cannot be pushed together under some new meta-narrative; three, everything appears as contingent; four, that which has had the greatest effect is the furthest away in time; five, no value appears as justifiable; six, in the deconstruction that follows everything appears as particular and immediate; seven, there are no universals; and eight, this outcome was contained as a possibility but not as a necessity in the social originary.

What follows from this is an immense social change and re-perception in which the age has to re-conceptualise itself on the basis of what has gone before while simultaneously no longer accepting what has gone before in its own terms. What shows up more specifically with respect to citizenship is that the concept appears as a false universal. It has been held together by mythical glue that has finally come unstuck.

Universalisation and Difference

There is a fundamental problem arising from the false universalism of citizenship concepts. The false universalism attributes general features to people which are too often remote from their real lives and excludes meaningful particular features of actual living. This abstraction ignores the actual identities of everyday life. In consequence it ignores issues of gender, race, and sexual orientation, to name a few. It is, instead, more concerned with the most general political categories. But the most general political categories by their generality and their universality cease to be political in a significant sense and are therefore remote from actuality. There are a variety of consequences that follow from this universality of citizenship concepts. Most obviously the categories within which people lead their lives and which are of most importance to them are inverted and appear as non-political. By contrast those engaged in a professional political life become, almost by definition and by common exclusion, an elite, but in doing so they become removed from much of the particularity of life. What ought to be political in the first case is excluded from politics, and what is apparently political in the second case becomes the politics of the abstract. A dismal view of this might take it that there is no politics at all.

The politics of the abstract depends for its viability on necessity in history, namely that occasion which determines the end(s) of history, the place in it at any particular time, and the broad position in its trajectory. So the apostles waited for the Second Coming of Christ, the *Parousia,* which was to occur in their lifetime, the Cargo cults waited for the messianic visit of silver aircraft and Marxists awaited the coming of the revolution. The universal significance of each of these individual and particular occasions was determined by the broader context. The end of the meta-narrative collapsed that broader context and with it the universal under which particularity was subsumed.

The consequence of the collapse of the universal was not the end of the particularity but rather the emergence of the particular as a factor in its own right. Without the broad over-arching context that explained, interpreted, subsumed and contained it, the particular emerged as difference. As difference, otherness, alterity, it became a prime political element: and one not dealt with by citizenship concepts as currently found. Those concepts turn out to be elitist, anti-political, falsely universalising or all three.

This raises the necessity of either abandoning citizenship concepts completely or finding a new viable conception of citizenship after the collapse of the grand meta-narratives. The complete abandonment of citizenship, while having its advocates, would lead ultimately to little more than selfishness, sectionalism and sectarianism – the three Ss that would be destructive of any programme or project of a shared world. In the rest of this section I will extend this diagnosis with the intention of unravelling some of its deeper components. I will show both the abstracting aspects of citizenship and the weaknesses that follow from that, while showing also that its universalistic pull, even in an age that appears to be anti-universalistic, is powerful, meaningful and significant.

I shall argue that there are powerful critiques against citizenship but nonetheless citizenship is an idea whose time has not yet run its course. In later chapters I will argue that even in a non-universalistic age it is possible to and necessary to 'act into the universal'. This notion will need some explanation but for now suffice to note that acting into the universal is based on the capacity of an enlarged mind to reach beyond the immediate. This capacity and its practice is empowering. I will extend this argument in two ways. I shall argue, first, that a citizenship of enlarged particularity is, within certain constraints, possible. Second, I shall argue that to act into the universal even to the point of self-annihilation is a kind of action that is not only built deeply into the tradition but is built into it in such a way that it can enhance significant dimensions of being.

The meta-narrative(s) within which citizenship has been comprehended have run across a variety of cultural expressions. In embryonic form it is part of the meta-narrative commencing with the earliest Mesopotamian assemblies of the pantheon. It is found later in the assemblies of the *polis* and yet later in the Roman Ecumene, in the Christian model of two cities, in the bourgeois split between 'man' and citizen and in the non-racial and non-gender category of citizen as currently found in some contemporary thought. Each of these ideas contains, however falsely it may subsequently appear, some account of the universal and all recognise the pull, power and significance of the universal.

At the same time there can be little argument with the proposition that citizenship concepts can abstract from everyday concerns to such an extent that citizenship risks becoming an abstraction itself. Marx put the difficulty well when he argued that 'Political emancipation is the reduction of man on the one hand, to a member of civil society, to an egoistic, independent individual and, on the other hand, to a citizen, a juridical person.'[9]

This difficulty is clear enough in the early bourgeois society which Marx took as his immediate target. The collapse of feudalism produced economically distinct individuals as the foundation of society. In their private economic relations they were, collectively, the components of civil society from which political relations were distinct. In such conditions the status of citizen was a gross abstraction – a mere juridical status. The citizen was the bearer of some rights and privileges and the bearer of a very few duties and obligations.

Such generality produced and produces little of distinctness between individual citizens. At its best it sets out what is common about people, what they share in some abstract sense. Its best feature is also its weakest feature for in its abstraction it is open to the critique that it ignores and cannot account for difference and otherness. As such differences become ever more important in the lives of people so conventional conceptions of citizenship are increasingly abstractions from those lives.

There is a clear problem here for if citizenship concepts are based on overly universalistic criteria they are nothing to the people involved. If, on the other hand, citizenship concepts were based on overly particularistic concerns then citizenship vanishes into the meaninglessness of excessive selfishness, sectionalism and sectarianism.

There is a legitimate question as to whether the elitism that springs from the universalising tendencies of citizenship concepts is just a contingent feature, or whether the problem goes deeper. The answer to the question depends on whether the elitism is historically or logically embedded. If the former, then its eradication depends on a radical change of historical conditions; if the latter, then its eradication depends on a radical rethinking of the concept of citizenship itself. I have argued that something like citizenship can be found in embryonic form in the social originary. I have also argued that while the social originary permits and depends on imaginings it does not follow from that observation that just any imagining is possible. Imaginings provide meaning and permit constructions but they permit constructions on something that is already found. They have limits provided by, among other things, what has gone before and the conditions in which we find ourselves. That we can legitimately construct such imaginings shows not so much the fertility of contemporary minds as the fertility and specificity of original sources.

Initially worldly citizenship was the construction that took place when heads of households gathered in a common place or domain acting in common ways independent of the tribe or household. Citizens are, as Aristotle emphasised in *The Politics,* members of a city. The coming together into a city was an act of belonging, of *synoicism.* That *synoicism* was later repeated in early Europe as an act of fraternity, or forswearing.[10] Acts of blood brotherhoods, found widely in early Europe, and similar forswearings are broadly equivalent. Such acts unite people who are not otherwise united by ties of kin or tribe. There is a strange and somewhat bizarre formal equivalent of this process found in some social contract theories and Voegelin writes in scathing terms about the bizarre forced *synoicism* found in Nehemiah's attempts to bring the Tribes of Israel together under one rubric – loyalty to one God.[11] The universal in that case was provided in the form of a religious rubric under which particularities were absorbed. The universal took an *a priori* form and did not arise from the particular activities or beliefs of the people involved.

By contrast a genuine unity between people takes natural and different units and creates commonalities and generalities over and above them. The *synoicism* is a practical matter, but it is one that can be justified in numerous ways, and one that can be completed or not. It is completed when the claims of the commonality build on the particularity of living and come to be seen as properly overriding other claims such as family or household. It is less than complete when those other claims continue to have the dominant hold. So when Pericles demanded and expected Athenians to lay down their lives, if necessary, in the service of Athens he made the political obligation of citizenship of Athens override familial claims. When Antigone died the public law was asserted. When Socrates took the hemlock he too accepted that the claims of the *polity* were greater than any individual preferences he might have. When Jesus accepted the cross he too accepted the public claims of the Roman Republic and when Bruni extolled the virtues of Florence he placed the public status of individuals as not dependent on their social status.

These are past examples but they are all the more significant for that, for they lay down, even sediment, the pattern of that which was to come. They are examples which are paradigmatic of the tension between the particular and the universal. That tension ultimately can be released only by sacrificing particular persons and acts into the universal. In each of these cases particularity is given an enlarged significance. Any model of the political nature of living and lives needs that characteristic if it is to avoid mere selfishness, mere sectionalism and mere sectarianism.

These examples, distant though they may be, are crucial for they show competing claims, competing desires, competing loyalties and even competing possibilities. Each one of the individuals involved could have chosen a different path. In each case they chose the path of following the public law, of reaching towards the general or universal and subsuming, not necessarily without regret, their particular concerns. Frequently they are tragic figures, but tragic figures with a point and a significance well beyond their immediate concerns. That people are willing to die for abstractions and perceived universalisations shows the power, the pull and the point of such abstractions in the real lives of particular people.

Examples of universalisation can be multiplied endlessly and found in various guises. The conclusions of such universalisations, if successful and not tautologically or analytically true, are powerful.

To show, for instance, that all individuals in one class are also members of another class is significant. To have shown that as all men are mortal any particular man is mortal is not trivial, and to show that each and every human is a citizen (if it were true) is not trivial. By itself, however, such a claim says nothing about lived experience. What, for instance, is the form of the mortality and the manner of dying. What is the activity of the citizen and what is its actuality? It is this kind of question that goes to the foundation of lived experience. Insofar as Socrates was mortal so he had to die. But this observation seems unimportant when set against the manner of his dying and its wider significance. In taking the hemlock in peace and tranquillity Socrates ended his life in a manner befitting that life. Similarly, that Jesus, taken by subsequent theological tradition as the incarnated Christ, showed that he was willing to live and to die as a mortal is a matter of significance far greater than his mortality *per se*.

The hemlock and the crucifixion are particular facts about the lives of Socrates and Jesus which matter in a way that their mortality does not. The one began the Western tradition of political obligation, the other the Christian theological tradition. In both cases the living and the manner of dying became definitive of a tradition. It was the particularities of living rather than the universality of category that was of prime significance.

This is not to say, however, that universals are worthless and that all argument and social concern should be in terms of particulars – far from it. To take that kind of view and only the particularities of life is what the early theologians called *hamartia*, or missing the mark. Expressed in theological terms, it became the concept of sin; its political equivalent is nihilism. So to show merely that Socrates took the hemlock is to show nothing of the universal dimensions of his life. And to show merely that Jesus died by crucifixion is to ignore the point of the incarnation and the universal component of that death. To miss the larger point of the death of Socrates is to miss the foundation of the Western theory of political obligation and to miss the second mark, the death of Jesus, is to miss the foundation of Western theology. Living straddles the larger dimensions of life as well as its more particular aspects. Concepts that deal with this must, if they are to be satisfactory, lie across both dimensions in adequate, if not always equal, measure.

Between Contingencies and Con Tricks

Zeno had a model of a city in which everyone would be equal. It is difficult to be sure who would be included for there is little of the account that is extant,[12] but as far as one can tell it included slaves and women. Its membership was truly universal. Zeno thought that the boundaries could be extended slowly so that more and more people would be absorbed into it. Ultimately the boundaries would be extended so far that it would include everyone – it would be a cosmic city. The sentiment is one of the finest expressed in political thought and in one way or another has influenced political thought through the ages. In early modern thought its equivalent is Dante's conception of *humanitas,* the view that everyone could be included into the category of humanity. It is a notion not to be thrown away lightly.

However, there is also a standard critique of both Zeno and of Dante that is powerful and telling. As Zeno's circles shift outwards so the differences between people become less and less apparent, and absorption depends on accepting the rules of the city. Ultimately there are no differences between people – they are all the same. This is the end point of universalisation: commonality without alterity, or universalisation without difference. The noble aim comes to undercut itself for it subsumes everything that counts in actual living under broad and finally meaningless categories.

A similar objection applies to Dante. Whose humanity is it that is being accepted and fostered? Dante took the Latin *humanitas,* a term that meant civility and manners, and gave it a new twist, turning it from its specific meaning of the manners of a particular people to the most general characteristics of all people. It was one of those rare moments in time when an old term, through desynonymisa-tion, the process of separating out a new meaning from a term with one original meaning, became the foundation of a completely new idea. Such opportunities are rare and Dante's use of the opportu-nity was brilliant and breathtaking in its scope. There were a few notable significant precedents. For example, St Augustine, towards the end of the Roman Empire, desynonymised the Latin term *voluntas.* This had been a legal interpretative term used to interpret an action of a defendant in a court. At that point there was no conception of free will. A court did not demand an account of action in such terms; it sought, rather, to understand the action against the backdrop of circumstances, the mental state of the defendant and so on. Augustine took the term *voluntas* and used it to introduce an entirely new idea, *voluntas* or will as an anthropological power. It is that idea which we now refer to as the power of freedom of the will. It was at this point and through the device of polysemy that a new and significant idea was introduced into the world. Polysemy is an important device. It is through this mechanism that many new concepts enter common currency. Gregory of Nyssa did it with *persona,* which he turned from the dramatic to the meta-physical idea of person; the idea of a being made in the image of

God and having a central core as opposed to a multitude of parts to play.[13]

Such moments are rare, they can also be of enormous significance. It is out of such polysemy that not only were new notions created but that new entities came into being: 'person', 'free will', and even 'human being' are not natural terms – they are inventions of a particular era that make sense primarily against a particular meta-narrative. These three concepts became interrelated and tied to the general meta-narrative in such a way that they reflect the core of the self-conceptions of an age; an age that came to have in it people of a certain sort. The people so conceived and self-reflected in that age are less natural entities than the contingent product of a set of historical circumstances. It is just a matter of accident or happenstance that the historical circumstances produced the concepts and the conditions for their transformation. The meta-narrative that provided the backdrop for their self-perception also turned out to produce self-descriptive and self-reflective concepts that were both universalising and which contained their own account of necessity within them.

So significant categories such as persons and human beings having the capacity of free will appeared as necessary features of beings made in the image of God and in the last days of history. To be a person in the image of God was more important than the particularities of lived life, for the real significance of being was in the imitation, not in the actuality of living. To be made in the image of God was definitive and essential, not mere happenstance. Similarly to have free will was to have a power of creation and the responsibility that went with that, a responsibility that would be met at the time of final judgment. The possession of free will became central to a major strand of Christian theology and of the political accounts of being and responsibility related to that.

This conception of necessity was possible and plausible because the meta-narrative within which the concepts developed was based on the apocalyptic-eschatological tradition as that was carried forward into Christian thinking. At its extreme the meta-narrative accounted for the actual living of someone by subordinating it to some larger end purpose. The beings that came into existence as a result of these transformations did not have merely the particular characteristics that any living being must have: they also had universal and general characteristics. Each of these characteristics, imitation, free will and humanity, became central to Western conceptions of humanity. In consequence to be human was to have certain characteristics defined in distinctively Western terms. These terms made sense only against the backdrop of a particular meta-narrative and a particular account of order, justice and appropriate behaviour.

Polysemy is a process by which new meanings, even new entities, come into being but it is not a process that is without its problems, in that new terms always carry part of their past connotations with them. In the case of humanity it carried with it, as part of its sediment or baggage, civility and manners. Civility and manners ultimately relate to behaviour and conduct, and an issue of significance that arises whenever conduct is considered as paradigmatic is whose behaviour and conduct is to count as the model? In consequence humanism contains the possibility of becoming not so much a genuine universalising category as yet another particularising category writ large. As Heidegger was right to point out, it is not that humanism is wrong *per se,* it is that in its previous conceptions it has been regarded in too small a way.[14]

In all these cases what is universalised is a particular category or experience. So, humanity in the large is understood in terms of Zeno's small city or Dante's conception of civility. Alternatively particular categories or experience might be left behind and new categories established. So citizenship in the *polis* emerged in a distinct public domain. The effect of that kind of universalisation was to leave partial interests behind. Affairs of the household, tribal matters, matters of the economy or of private trade, or social or personal matters had, with rare exceptions, no place in the *polis.* No one concerned with household affairs – women or slaves, for example – had any public and therefore any citizenship status or powers.

Particularising trends and tendencies take many forms. The list is almost endless[15] for people live particular lives, they do not live in abstract categories and all too often the abstract categories are used to rob people of their lived lives. The phenomenon is not new. The ancient peasant was not enfranchised for he was a citizen of heaven. The slave, as even St Paul pointed out, was equal in the sight of God – but still, and properly so, a slave on earth. The women was a sexual repository, a chattel or a thing, or all three. By making apparently universal categories the categories of prime importance and then making the categories exclusive anyone excluded was excluded from what was important in life. Similarly to exclude a particular activity or set of activities from citizenship is to remove real concerns from its purview. The women of the household in Ancient Greece were excluded from citizenship by virtue of their sexuality but their activities were also excluded by virtue of being social rather than political.

This is not confined to early examples. The women of Europe and North America were until recently disenfranchised by virtue of their sexuality. Similarly issues pertaining to gender, race, and many social and economic activities are excluded from the universalising effects of citizenship. These latter concerns raise issues of individuality and particularity, but it is these that are most often what matter to people in their actual living. This produces tension arising from opposing tendencies. The scope of citizenship has been limited in two marked ways. The first is in limitations on membership found in the notion of citizenship, while the second is the limitation that is placed on what might count as civic activity. Set against that has been the collapse of the meta-narratives, and other constraining devices that legitimated the limitations on the scope of citizenship. The effect of that collapse has been to release issues of gender, race, ethnicity and other particularities as central to, rather than peripheral to, politics. The very characteristics of individual lived identity that were excluded by citizenship have become the central feature of the increasingly important politics of identity. The politics of the particular rather than the politics of the universal has become a major characteristic of the politics of our time. As citizenship, from its inception, has been concerned with the general or universal, it seems irrelevant to the particularities generated by this life politics.

Nowhere is the politics of the particular more evidenced than in the contemporary requirement to have a personal identity of one's own. The developing importance of personal identity is no mere whim but is the consequence of the collapse of the general structures within which living and personality were placed into and drawn from a wider context. Traditional structures provided general meaning and a place within that. Its clearest point was in the idea of the right order or the great chain of being in which individuality and personality were subsumed to some cosmic design. The place for the individual is expressed well in the idea of 'my station and its duties', which is found in a variety of forms both ancient and modern.

By contrast the contemporary notion of having a personal identity is of an identity developed in the context of real life situations and not in the abstraction of general or universal categories provided by the meta-narrative of some artificially provided history. It is made, not imposed. Such a conception of personal identity formed in the absence of fixed structures and fixed stories thrusts people onto their own resources. Inevitably they will look for, and attempt to create, meaning locally; that is to say in particular situations. In that context abstract categories are relatively meaningless.

To the extent that citizenship is only, or primarily, a universalising concept it will be placed under strain and will seem meaningless, insignificant, trivial, irrelevant, politically neutering or all of these. The difficulty that the concept of the citizen faces in these respects goes back to its roots. If we look once again into that aspect of the strange but intriguing quasi-historical and less than glassy pool that reveals fragments of moments in the social originary, we see the gods in assembly. But if we look further, behind the assembly, we see that the gods have concerns of their own that they do not always bring to the assembly. Even the gods, its seems, have particular concerns. The examples of the gods are repeated endlessly: so, for example, in Athens tribal interests dominated to the point where Solon, that wisest of Archons, had to balance competing tribal and class interests to save the *polis*.

It is clear that there is a series of problems right at the heart of citizenship concepts. Citizenship concepts as traditionally conceived miss the point of people's lives, for they are universalising at the expense of giving due weight to living categories and living experiences. The classical response to this has been to invoke the meta-narrative within which individual lives make some kind of larger sense against the backdrop of a right order. When people are told stories of that kind they accept that the prime category to which they belong is a universal one. But when the pillars on which such meta-narratives rest collapse, so life has to be led in terms found in its actuality and in its particularity. In that case citizenship appears not so much a device that is enfranchising and liberating as a device that in disguised, yet startlingly effective, form is at the foundation of the political castration of a population. That political castration is partly a consequence of the nature of the concept of the citizen and partly a consequence of its deliberate misuse.

At that point the social originary comes to be seen for what it is: a mirror that shows us why we are where we are. When it shimmers, distorts or even breaks we see that we are in a strange, important, and illusory world that lies somewhere between a set of contingencies and a set of con tricks.

3

The Looking-Glass Culture

I argued in the previous chapter that the universalising tendency of citizenship concepts results in those concepts being removed from important features and aspects of actual living. It is often maintained that there is a distinction between active and passive citizenship that ought to avoid this difficulty by permitting people as active citizens to be engaged in their own lives. The distinction between active and passive citizenship ought to invoke quite different concepts and carry two quite different ideas about world engagement with them. It ought, therefore, to deal with the problems that have turned up at the very centre of the idea of citizenship. I will argue that it has not and cannot achieve this aim, for the distinction between active and passive citizenship is itself weak.

The reason for this weakness is that the scope or domain across which the notion of active and passive citizenship applies is sufficiently similar that it overrides whatever basic distinctions might otherwise obtain between these concepts. Put starkly there is little point in being an active citizen if there is no domain in which that citizenship can be effectively acted out. These actual limits to a significant practical domain for the effective exercise of citizenship result in a blurring of the distinctions between active and passive citizenship. This is not to say that there are no distinctions between active and passive citizenship. There are, but for some people only. In most cases the reality is that active citizenship is a chimera and in some cases that chimera is such that it disguises the effect of citizenship as a device for subsuming people in the twin prisons of subjection and subjectivity.

Citizenship is an idea containing a radical potential for empowerment, but if that potential is to be realised the traditional distinction between active and passive citizenship will need to be bypassed. I will later argue that this is possible and that citizenship can be utilised in an empowering way, but if this is to be the case the concepts of politics and of citizenship will need to be radically different from the politics and citizenship of the past. This will require some account of the recovery of politics and in the next chapter I will examine that idea. I want here to show how in many cases citizenship is effectively subjection.

The Occasional and Shallow Citizen

It is generally admitted that citizenship concepts distinguish between active and passive citizenship. I will argue that this distinction is itself shallow and that both concepts of citizenship draw the domain of action in such a restricted way that citizenship comes to be perceived as irrelevant to lived concerns. One consequence of that restriction is that citizenship is seen to be additional to, rather than integral to, life. In consequence the larger concerns and implications of individual actions are frequently under-considered. This can lead to a perception of action as merely individual, private and non-political rather than relating it to others and world as a form of shared world engagement.

The distinction between active and passive citizenship is usually conceived as a reasonably clear one that goes right to the foundation of citizenship arguments. Active citizenship is found in that model imaged in the pantheon, and derived from the *polis*.[1] It was found among the higher classes in Rome, in attenuated form in some of the early European saga cultures,[2] re-created in the medieval cities in Germany[3] and in Italy of the *Quattrocentro*. It is repeated as an idea by the early English humanists,[4] in the federalism of the founding fathers, and in the Republican tradition generally. In the twentieth century it has found a strong expression in English Idealism,[5] in the republican revival,[6] in Arendt,[7] who makes action in the public realm the source of individual distinctness, and in some aspects of the democratic project[8] or radical democracy.

On the face of it active citizenship encourages political activity and political responsibility. It is the model of shared world engagement. Some thinkers have taken this kind of political world engagement to be so important that they have made it the centre of human being. Notable as a turning point in this respect was William of Moerbecke's translation of Aristotle's *Ta Politika*, *The Politics*. In that translation he provided the concept of *polistheuma* which in Dante's thought became *politizare*; acting politically as the very centre of humanity. The thought is not entirely new, although it does mark a change in thinking, nor does it start or end with Dante. For Aristotle man was *zoon politikon*, and for Bruni and later republicans to be active in the city was to develop one's finest faculties. What Dante did provide, however, was a conception that freely willing, that activity which had led to the Fall, was not an activity to be regretted, but an activity to be celebrated. The Fall was definitive of what it was to be human. To will and to be engaged in making and re-making one's own life was, therefore, to be human. At its best active citizenship as world engagement with others is definitive of humanity. Its loss or its significant diminution is therefore a loss of or diminution of humanity.

To be a passive citizen might mean one of two things. It might be merely to have a status as member, subject to laws and having some protection by a political community. Alternatively it might be the obverse side of active citizenship, as when, for instance, the status instead of the activity of a citizen is referred to. Rousseau and Kant draw attention to this latter distinction when they talk about one and the same person being head and member of a political association.[9] In this latter sense the relation between a passive and an active citizen is one of aspect or imaging. Looked at in one way the citizen is active, looked at in another way the citizen is passive. In this sense necessarily all active citizens are also passive citizens having a status, but the converse is not true. Some passive citizens are denied the status of active citizenship.

The *locus classicus* of the second model is found in the citizenship granted to the peoples of the Roman Empire who fell outside the ruling class.[10] They had status and protection but were not entitled to and not fit to participate in political activity. This created a set of citizens that were active and a set of citizens that were passive having merely status. In its more extreme expression this is the creation of subjects. Passive citizenship as little more than subjection is found in Kant,[11] and the aftermath to the French Revolution, while in Hobbes and Burke,[12] and in much early liberal thought, the passive status is one of subjection where a subject is one that has a certain status that includes obedience to and protection of the state but where having that status does not automatically invoke a right to either general or particular political activity.[13] The status of passive citizen or of subject may invoke permission to engage in some minimal political activity i.e. the right to vote for a representative[14] while not permitting one to be a representative oneself, or it may even deny that right, by contenting itself with the claim that citizenship is a mere attribution of status.[15]

Such status is not necessarily meaningless as the arrest of St Paul in Jerusalem in the first century graphically shows. According to Luke, confusion in Jerusalem was caused by the reaction to Paul's appearance at the Temple. A Tribune sought out the confusion and had his soldiers bind Paul with two chains. The Tribune commanded that Paul be examined with scourges to determine the extent of his crime. As they stretched him, Paul said to the centurion:

'If a man is a Roman citizen and uncondemned is it lawful for you to scourge him?' ...

And approaching Paul the tribune said to him, 'Tell me are you a Roman?'

And he said, 'Yes' ...

Those about to examine him moved immediately away from him as did the Tribune who was afraid knowing fully that he had bound a Roman citizen.[16]

The incident shows just how important the status of citizenship might be and there are numerous eloquent attestations to it. These range from the rousing claims of Pericles in *The Funeral Oration* through to its echo by Bruni in the Florentine Republican revival of the *Quattrocentro*. Bruni advocated the opportunity to engage in political activity while nevertheless extolling the benefits of citizenship status:

> ... a certain balance among the various ranks was created, since the great can rely on their power, the small on the common-wealth and both on the fear of punishment to deter transgressors. From this the saying was born, which we hear most frequently hurled against the powerful, for when they threaten something, the cry goes up at once 'I, too, am a Florentine citizen!' By this saying they seem to be attesting and publicly warning that no one should despise anybody on account of his weakness, nor continue to threaten injury by exploiting his own power; that the situation of everyone is the same, since those with less power will be avenged by the commonwealth itself.[17]

The status of the citizen may be extended from the merely passive form of protection to the formal activity of voting while nevertheless denying any meaningful form of political activity. A life without a stake in the political community is a life that may be accompanied by an inability to partake in that community either politically or economically.

There are two cases of the relation between active and passive citizen: one in which both conditions are held in one and the same person and the other in which they are held separately. In some cases the relation between active and passive citizen will be an exclusive one. In such a case to be one is not, at least not simultaneously, to be the other. When Rousseau distinguishes between citizen and subject in one and the same person,[18] and Kant distinguishes between the head and member of a city,[19] they point to the impossibility of simultaneously holding all the characteristics of activity and passivity. The action is undertaken as an active citizen, but the effect of the action is temporally successive to the performance of the action. It is received as a passive citizen or even as a subject.

Once again aspect is important, for in both cases Rousseau and Kant seem to assume that it is the same person that is involved, but in each case the image in the mirror is slightly different. From the perspective of the person the mental state must be different. For an action to be a political action or for an event to be a political event it must have a relevant meaning and intentional structure. To distinguish between active and passive citizens in one and the same person requires a fairly sophisticated underpinning that relates meaning, intention, social structure and events together.

Another kind of distinction between active and passive citizens is, on the face of it, more marked. It is when the distinction between active and passive citizen is not made in one and the same person but when it is made between different persons or, more generally, between different classes of person. There are various precedents for this. The most marked was in Rome where, while many were citizens of some kind, only some classes of people, the patricians, were able to take an active role in the political life of the republic. Others were excluded from this. They might, and did have, the protection of the republic, and they did owe duties to the republic, but they did not participate in its decision-making process. Cicero, for example, thought it right that the 'vulgar and odious trades' should be excluded from participation in the public realm, as participation required the values of a liberal education, with the carefulness of thought and the art of rhetoric that could be developed through such an education. But the distinction does not stop at Rome. It turns up, surprisingly in a way, in Immanuel Kant, an egalitarian about many things, who argued that:

> The capacity to vote is a prerequisite of being a citizen. To have such a capacity presupposes that a person is politically independent not just as an incidental part of the commonwealth, but also as a member of it, that is, one who, together with others, acts in accordance with his own will, as an active part of the commonwealth. This last qualification leads to the distinction between an active and a passive citizen ...[20]

On this model, to be politically independent was not to be under the command of another as a ploughman or servant would be, but to have the kind of autonomous skills that a carpenter or skilled tradesman would have. That he defines independence in a way entirely supportive of his case and that his case distinguishes between the bourgeoisie and those under their domination does not strike him as odd. Usually the clearest of thinkers on this issue, he was, in this case, both partial and woolly minded.

What seemed to Kant to be of no importance, just as it seemed to be of no importance to Cicero, was that to have a stake in the polity or state or republic requires not merely that one is under its protection and has its status, valuable though that might be, but that one also has a meaningful and significant involvement in its decisions: to be, in contemporary jargon, a stake-holder. The principle, if not the term, of stake-holding had been recognised as early as Solon who, when faced with an Athens that was tearing itself apart under the effects of a class war, gave every member of the *polis* a stake in its decision-making. All members of differing classes were brought into the decision-making process and granted protection in a careful social and political balance. I quote at some length from Solon and from some expressions of similar sentiment across the ages.

> I gave to the mass of the people such rank as befitted their need,
> I took not away their honour, and I granted naught to their greed;
> But those who were rich in power, who in wealth were glorious and great,
> I bethought me that naught should befall them unworthy their splendour and state;
> And I stood with my shield outstretched, and both were safe in its sight.
> And I would not that either should triumph, when the triumph was not with right.[21]

The same principle that participation in decision-making regardless of social status was significant, possible and desirable was repeated in Pericles' *The Funeral Oration,* where it was declared that:

> If we look to the laws, they afford equal justice to all in their private differences; if to social standing, advancement in public life falls to reputation for capacity, class considerations not being allowed to interfere with merit; nor again does poverty bar the way, if a man is able to serve the state, he is not hindered by the obscurity of his condition.[22]

The sentiment, even the formula, is repeated in that famous echo of Pericles' panegyric given by Bruni. In his own panegyric he praises Solon, and then the general Nanni Strozzi, who died in the service of Florence.

> The hope of attaining office and of raising oneself up is the same for all, provided, only one put in effort and have talent and a sound and serious way of life. Virtue and probity are required of the citizens by our city. Anyone who has these two qualities is thought to be sufficiently well-born to govern the republic.[23]

To have a stake in the realm or the *common weale* is not merely to have a full economic stake in it but to have the opportunity to play a part in its decision-making. This comes through appropriate citizenship. In its earliest modern form the principle was recognised well by Marsilius of Padua who declared that:

> The absolutely primary human authority to make or establish human laws belongs only to those men from whom alone the best laws can emerge. But these are the whole body of citizens, or the weightier part thereof.[24]

'The whole body of citizens' excluded women – thus once again continuing the exclusivity of the concept.

The distinction between active and passive citizenship operates in two different ways. It may occur in different aspects of the same person, as when the same person is also subject to the legislation that they have enacted. Alternatively the distinction may refer to two different people or classes or types of people, as with Cicero's cultured and odious people, Kant's active and passive citizens or the duality of citizenship established after the French Revolution fell away from its early ideals. In the last two cases some will be active or entitled to be active in the manufacture of decisions while others will not. They may even be formally excluded from action on grounds of personal type, class or wealth. The odious, the dependent and the poor have in such cases the status of citizen and the protection that comes from that, but they do not constitute that part of the domain which has the authority to make laws.

There is a clear, formal and sometimes substantive distinction between active and passive citizenship that stretches back for more than two millennia. It is a distinction presented in various forms and remains reasonably sharp until the domain in which active citizens have little more effective authority to make or participate in the making of laws than passive citizens is severely restricted or even eliminated. At that point the distinction between active and passive citizens is little more than a juridical notion: it is not a practical or effective distinction.

This distinction occurs most clearly when the scope of citizenship is restricted. If nominally active citizens are denied an effective domain of action then their active citizenship is practically and effectively worthless. For active citizenship to be meaningful and distinguishable from mere status it is necessary that such citizens are provided with a scope within which their permitted activities make a significant difference to the way they lead their lives. Frequently it does not, for the bounds of the public domain are often drawn in ways that restrict the perception of the *common weale* and the players on its stage.

A related but somewhat different problem arises when the narrow outlook which may come from living a restricted and narrow life and from being excluded from wider concerns of the conditions of living is brought to the public domain and then comes to dominate its concerns. The particular subsumes the common and active citizenship is concerned only with the immediacies arising from status. The end point of that narrow domination is sectarianism, sectionalism and selfishness, characteristics that are inimical to citizenship but which may pass as its false and potentially damaging substitute.

If citizenship, acting politically, as with William of Moerbecke's *polistheuma* or Dante's *politizare*, is important to the development of *humanitas* then it may be that citizenship as currently construed cannot deliver what it might be thought to promise. A source of that limitation might be that in the absence of a meaningful scope for significant and distinct public action the difference between active and passive citizenship is damagingly limited. It may even be so limited that citizenship turns into subjection.

Who Do We See in the Mirror?

To be a subject might mean one of several things. It might mean that one is a subject of consciousness, that powerfully strange form of mental state crystallised by Augustine and Descartes. Here, to use the Cartesian formula, mind is a single substance. It might mean alternatively that one is a subject of a kingdom, a prince, a monarch or a state. In the second case it refers to a political rather than to a mental state. Looked at from one aspect these conditions are quite different: the mental subject in its Cartesian substantial formula is significantly prior to the world in which they live, while the earthly subject is subordinate to the state. They are, looked at from another aspect, quite similar. Being is subject to its own subjectivity. It might be developed, modified, changed in some ways, certainly affirmed but it is a subjection of a kind. Hence the cries of lamentation from those who find themselves a prisoner of a consciousness with which they are not comfortable, or the screams of angst and torment from those who find themselves with a consciousness which they cannot respect in any way.

It is not surprising that the relation between the inner and outer sometimes finds itself expressed in the language of subjection and subjectivity. Self and culture are inter-related, inter-twined and inter-imagined as part of the same larger social imaginary. When, to recur to an earlier metaphor, the facing mirrors are perfectly aligned we see ourselves infinitely presented and re-presented but from a different aspect. If there were no change of aspect there would be no sense of self. To have a perfect image of ourselves in our culture would be to have no sense of self at all. To exist and to subsist we need to see something that is not quite ourselves. Sometimes we see some *thing* that we scarcely recognise at all as a *who*. This radical *heteronomia* is a significant political challenge, for when it occurs others appear as objects or as strangers. This might produce an intolerance to radically different images and with it the preclusion of the coming together of different people in the *demos*. The danger of that is the rise of particularity writ large as if it were a universal.

Subjection and subjectivity are built into citizenship concepts and are internal and external aspects of each other. Breaking the mould of subjection in the political sense is tied, therefore, to breaking the mould of subjectivity in the mental sense. Formally active yet effectively shallow citizenship fosters subjectivity/subjection. This is markedly the case when the citizen has no effective domain or space within which to operate. In such cases even the active citizen becomes passive or subjective. This is added to when there is no appropriate mental set which could lead individual actions to be regarded as political actions except in the most limited way and on the most limited of occasions: the formality of voting for instance. This formal and restricted sense of what counts as an appropriate civic activity may well serve to increase the elitism in citizenship.

The elitism in citizenship, and therefore the associated increase in subjection and subjectivity, might be quite noticeable. For Aristotle citizenship excluded slaves, woman and aliens, for Cicero it excluded those of the vulgar trade even while they might be passive citizens; for Kant it excluded those who were merely tradesmen[25] even though they were nominally passive citizens; and for all the noble ideals of the French Revolution, where equal rights were guaranteed for all on a sacred basis, it came to exclude those who could not afford and therefore were not worthy of full recognition.[26]

This is not to say that status citizenship has been or even now is unimportant. But its importance re-enforces its subjection and its effects on subjectivity. To be stateless in the contemporary world and therefore to be a permanent subject of nowhere is to be diminished as a human being. This observation holds not merely of the present: it held also of the past, as shown, for example, in the respect accorded to St Paul. Full citizenship has sometimes been expanded, granted as an honour or reward for noble action, a practice found as early as Ancient Greece. It might be acquired through adoption, a practice found rarely in Greece, but more frequently in Rome or by incorporation into a relevant and appropriate religion.[27] Status citizenship might be bought, as the Tribune who arrested St Paul bought his citizenship of Rome. It is not surprising that people will go to considerable lengths to acquire even minimal status citizenship. It offers protection, economic possibilities and the chance of an escape from the worst ravages of the chattel status, bondage, guest worker status, illegal immigrancy and countless other disgraces and inhumanities.[28]

In an imperfect world, status citizenship is invaluable. It governs and regulates numerous cases of different kinds of action, as does passive citizenship or that form of mere subjectivity that is equivalent to subject citizenship and that is found in, for instance, Hobbes. Even here it is not worthless for it offers the protection of the Leviathan and the opportunity to engage in the economic activities of civil society. Contrary to popular myth, the Leviathan, while having a remarkable degree of informal control, is formally prescriptive but not formally proscriptive to any great lengths. The Leviathan sets limits but does not, outside those limits, prescribe action(s). Such subject/citizenship excludes, therefore, the populace at large from the quasi-political domain of the Leviathan while permitting activities that lie outside that domain as it is tightly drawn. The message is almost a paradigm of contemporary citizenship. It is as if the maxim 'Do what you will but do not trespass into the public domain' (a domain defined by the Leviathan or by the state) operates.

These relations and considerations might seem archaic and irrelevant. So they would be if they were not definitive of a significant part of the modern European state, especially as that has been developed in the United Kingdom, and if they did not continue into contemporary subjection. The relation between subjectivity and subjection is not accidental. It is found in its most marked and most extreme form in Thomas Hobbes, where the very condition of consciousness is to be subordinated to the Leviathan, the state. Under the power of the Leviathan to provide the 'apt imposition of names', language itself and its meaning is controlled. Given the relation between language and thought, those who are subjects of the Leviathan are also subject to the Leviathan. In that act of subjectionivity (subjection/subjectivity), politics and citizenship are terminated and society and potential political activity is subordinated to the activity of the state in an absolutist gesture that surpasses all understanding.

In this model, citizenship is so passive that it is merely subjection. This Hobbesian position seems radically different from those models that take citizenship as active, significant and meaningful. Yet the distinction between subjectivity and subjection and passive and active citizenship is not always that clear cut. Even active citizenship is useless if it has no domain into which it can act. And this is precisely its weakness.

The weakness can be so marked that active citizenship may, for all practical purposes, be equivalent to passive citizenship. And passive citizenship may be no more than status subjection. The inability of the active citizen to be a citizen in all but name, or in all but formal activities, might be, and often is, so complete and passive that it is effectively and formally equivalent to mere subjectivity.

Status citizens or subjects or citizen/subjects may obtain some form of protection while having duties that are not personally enhancing. They may even find that the limited quasi-political activity of voting is restricted or non-existent while their other political requirements are significant and even run in the face of their basic culture. Australian Aborigines are a case in point,[29] as are the indigenous people referred to by Kymlicka.[30] But if the domain or place or space within which active citizenship can be exercised is effectively lacking then active citizenship is merely an empty formula and the active citizen has, in practice, only the status, duties and rights of a passive citizen. In turn the passive citizen may be merely a subject, of consciousness and of state.

The implication of this is that active and passive citizens are effectively equivalent to passive citizens. Of course some people do attempt to participate in what passes for the public domain but this merely perpetuates the sham. Similarly in many cases active and passive citizens are effectively equivalent to mere subjects, in both senses, and this continues the sham even further, for what appears as a liberating idea is a constraining idea. Citizenship may provide the *idea* of participation in one's own life decisions at the public level while restricting real activity. Citizenship, as found hitherto, is exclusive and elitist instead of inclusive and egalitarian. It is the very opposite of what it promises. What it promises is a particular and strong conception of what it is to be human and a place and opportunity within which to exercise that capacity. What it has delivered is the twin prisons of subjectivity and subjection.

The Broken Mirror or Democracy by Nobody

The effect of much citizenship arguments and programmes has been the creation of what is a citizen subject: someone who is nominally a citizen but who is in actuality a subject in the twin senses of subjectivity and subjection. In Western democracies the members rarely have the merely formal status, such of *de jure* subjection without the accompanying *de jure* status of citizenship. Nonetheless some kind of *de facto* subjection, or effectively limited citizenship is widespread even in Western liberal democracies.

There are a number of ways in which that effective subjection can be developed, ranging from the fairly minor to the more serious and on into the kind of problems identified in the previous sections that are so fundamental that they throw the entire idea of citizenship into question. The minor and trivial obstacles to an effective citizenship might be having restricted gateways to public life, placing excessively difficult hurdles in the way of effective participation, excessive bureaucracy and similar problems which individually are surmountable but which collectively generate an anti-participatory ethos. More serious problems arise from making the hurdles impossible to surmount in practice so that there is a claim to openness while the actuality is the opposite. Any mechanism that claims openness while providing a severely restricted actual access to public life produces effective second-class citizenship.

Representative democracies often tend to institutionalise such second-class citizenship by structurally denying the possibility of general and widespread participation. Representatives, in acting for, or representing, the views of others, necessarily limit direct participation. The end result is that for most citizens in representative democracies, political activity is not a significant or meaningful part of their lives. A common consequence of that limitation is the view that politics has no part in their lives and that it is a generally disreputable and limited activity in which they have no interest. The upshot is political apathy. This can be turned around and presented as a virtue, as it is whenever the claim is made that liberal representative democracies require large amounts of political apathy for their continuance.

An ameliorating argument is frequently offered to the effect that, notwithstanding this apathy, the level of political activity that liberal democracies do have is greater than in some other previous models; absolutism for instance. In liberal democracies, while there is little individual direct activity in the state, nevertheless some political activity is permitted. With a few exceptions, all the adult population is permitted to vote and enter the formal political forum as a representative.

Of course not everyone can be a representative and all such models of government while nominally open are simultaneously and effectively closed to large proportions of the population. Representation is a gateway through which only a few people can pass. In principle everyone has the formal right to be a representative, but as the number of representatives at any one time is severely curtailed so necessarily not everyone can be a representative. If political activity is defined in terms of the professional political activity that occurs in the central public forum, then the restriction on political activity is limited. This limitation occurs not merely as a matter of practice but as a matter of necessity.

There is an additional difficulty arising from this restriction. A representative is not engaged in the forum in their own right but always as standing for, or standing in for, someone else. That someone else is not an actual person but a set of people. The representative is not, therefore, present in their own right but in the place of some other person. That other person, however, turns out to be not another actual individual but a group of individuals. The representative, it seems, acts not for themselves and represents no actual person. Who then is the representative culture and who and what is it that is represented?

The sceptical response is that there is only a model person, a representative, but not an actual person that is acting in the public domain. Relatedly there is no actual person that is represented, for the representation is of kind or type, and not of an instance. If this *reductio* is followed through, it would seem that whatever a representative model of politics models it is not politics and relatedly that the representative model of politics does not permit actual politics. Hence there is no politics in contemporary democracies. This is a conclusion that is neither unusual nor surprising. The representative model of politics clearly disallows either a genuinely agonistic or a genuinely direct form of politics but insofar as something like that kind of activity does occur it is, as the term suggests, a model.

The representative model of government in its pure form is depoliticising. As this is a structural objection, the recovery of politics would have to occur outside formal state structures. There is a prior issue that requires discussion, namely the limits placed on consciousness as a consequence of the twin prisons of subjectivity and subjection. Without some possibility of escape from those twin prisons any attempt to remodel politics, no matter how dramatic and radical it might be, would amount to little more than tokenism. Clearly, given the relation between self and world, there are not two separate issues to be dealt with: a modified consciousness and a modified politics. They are interrelated and a change of one is only possible in the context of a change of the other. Nonetheless if some changes in consciousness of a certain kind are not possible then some related changes in political form are unlikely to occur.

To break from the twin prisons of subjectivity and subjection requires a change in both the way we think and the way we think about ourselves – a break in consciousness and a change in the way we act and perceive our actions. Citizenship as hitherto construed has subsumed subject and citizen in each other as twin subjects.

There is a long and clear recognition of the relation between citizenship and consciousness. Citizenship is taken to be ennobling, as part of what is required for full development, as a means of raising consciousness. The ideal of the civic virtues, the idea of serving the city, are continually praised throughout the history of citizenship. There are hints of some understanding of the relation between consciousness in the form of pride and the civic life in Solon, it is evident in Pericles, and central in Aristotle. For Bruni, writing at the dawn of the age of modern consciousness, the relation between mind and citizenship is intimate:

> ... the only legitimate constitution left is the popular one, in which liberty is real, in which legal equity is the same for all citizens, in which pursuit of the virtues may flourish without suspicion. And when a free people are offered this possibility of attaining offices, it is wonderful how effectively it stimulates the talents of the citizens. When shown a hope of gaining office, men rouse themselves and seek to rise; when it is precluded they sink into idleness.[31]

An obvious consequence of this is that citizenship ought to be expanded to as many as possible. It was a consequence that was rarely observed. It never seemed to occur to Cicero that those who were condemned to be in the 'odious occupation of the collector of customs, and the usurer and the base and menial work of unskilled labourers,'[32] could have benefited from a liberal education and the practice of office. Even Kant, more than anyone else the philosopher of consciousness, did not see the mind-limiting consequences of his distinction between active and passive citizens. Ironically it was Robespierre who most clearly saw the aims of the Revolution despoiled by this kind of distinction. In an outburst in the Assembly he said: 'Do you honestly believe that a hard, laborious life engenders as many vices as one of comfort, luxury and ambition?'[33]

The examples of the ennobling effects of the civic virtues can be multiplied endlessly, but the related observation that the opportunity to practice such virtues should be widely available is relatively rare. Similarly the connection between civic virtue and mental enlargement is rarely used to explain the reverse observation that might have been made, namely, the high number of 'odious people'.

To some extent that kind of connection had to await the discovery of the 'modern mind'. Only if the mind is perceived in dynamic terms related to its conditions is it possible to perceive that mass exclusion from the possibility of practising the civic virtues is the cause rather the consequence of the 'odious'. And only if the mind is perceived as having an inner space of its own does the relation between individual consciousness and external action and circumstance make clear sense. The inter-reflexive observation that 'I am in the world and the world is in me' does not collapse world and self: it interrelates them. It is an observation that, so interpreted, is characteristic of the modern mind in the modern world.

The idea of the modern mind can be stretched back to a time before modernity. It is certainly evident in early form in St Augustine's account of his mental journey as presented in *The Confessions*; it recurs endlessly after that in accounts of journeys, visions, dreams and vistas in which the individual mind plays a part. It is no accident that it turns up in Dante not merely as travail but as love story and it is no accident that in one of its most poignant expressions it turns up in Rousseau's *Confessions*. In all such cases it is the inner and individual space of the modern mind that is being exhibited.

Such romanticism is not far from citizenship. Indeed it is closely related. Augustine turned from the confessions to the two cities and to an account of citizenship on earth and in heaven. Dante invoked the idea of *politizare*, of acting in this world and taking pleasure in just that central aspect of humanity, and Rousseau placed being a citizen as central to morality and morality as required for humanity. The connection is not accidental, for in both cases love dominates. It is, first, romantic love and then it is the love of the world and both are simultaneously possible because of the mental space that the former exhibits and the latter demands and creates.

This is to say that self and world are twin aspects of the mental space of the modern mind. It is also to say that one cannot be fully experienced without the other. The next step in the development is to enlarge both without sinking into egoism. Dante and the civic humanists took the formal first step, but it was, ironically yet appropriately, Immanuel Kant who more than anyone else provided the formal mechanism for enlargement of the mind. Ironically, for the emotion of romantic love seems to have been absent from his experience; appropriately, for he was the formal philosopher of consciousness *par excellence*.

The crucial turning point in Kant's philosophy is, from this respect, not to be found in his earlier critiques on knowledge and practical reason but in his later and almost unread *The Third Critique, The Critique of Judgement*. I will pick out two components of that which will recur in various forms throughout this argument. The first is the distinction that he draws between a determinative and a reflective judgment. A determinative judgment occurs when a case requiring a judgment falls under a pre-existing rule or set of rules. That judgment is made by the application of pre-existing rules. To take a mundane example: if I buy some goods at the supermarket I apply at the till a set of rules already present. Such rules relate to exchange models, payment, conventions about manners and so on. These are complex but I have learnt them and, having learnt them, they are neither debatable, negotiable or otherwise challengeable. Nor, and this is significant, are they mind enhancing.

By contrast if I am walking in the countryside and a flying saucer lands next to me and a little green person emerges from it and seeks my help in escaping from a peculiar Martian dilemma, I am likely to be flummoxed, partly by the situation and partly because I do not comprehend the dilemma or its full significance. Some judgment is required but clearly it is not a ready-made determinative judgment. Such a judgment is a reflective judgment, it applies when there is no clear rule available to which I can appeal. The difference between these two forms of judgment is marked and fundamental. In the first case I move from the general or universal (the rule) to the particular (the circumstance). In the second I am compelled to move from the particular (the case that I find) to the universal (which I do not know). Put in non-Kantian terms which I will use later, I act towards or into the universal.

The second component of note in *The Third Critique* is the modification that Kant makes of the imperatives made in his earlier practical philosophy. These imperatives, the Categorical Imperatives, placed absolute moral injunctions on autonomous agents – which is to say all rational beings. The central force of the modification is that in acting one ought to seek to examine a situation from the viewpoint of others.

The first of these conditions, reflective judgment, requires a morally enlarged mind if it is to be met; the second requires the practice of that morally enlarged mind with respect to social situations. Both recur in later thinkers: the first in Arendt's theory of judging, which she regards as the most political of our mental faculties, and the second in Habermas's 'Discourse Ethics'.

What emerges from this is that the modern mind and the modern political condition are intimately related. That relation is certainly trailed in embryonic form in Augustine, in more developed form in Dante's twin conceptions of *politizare* and *humanitas,* and in Rousseau's relation between political participation, morality and humanity. But it is also more specifically and formally worked out in Kant's *The Third Critique* and the political appropriations that have followed from that. The enlargement of the mind requires the exercise of reflective judgment and the consideration of situations from the perspectives of others. Such an outlook is ineluctably and ineradicably political and such a practice is at the root of the recovery of the civic virtues.

Such an outlook is also at the root of breaking free of the twin prisons of subjection and subjectivity. The enlargement of the mind is a route to a condition beyond mere mental subjection, requiring opportunity, circumstance and practice. To look at situations from the point of view of others requires that there be others with perspectives sufficiently different from one's own as to make the enterprise reasonable and worthwhile. It would seem that the enlargement of mind requires alterity and alterity produces new circumstances that invoke reflective judgment, that most political of our mental faculties. That too feeds mental and political enlargement. The concept of self and citizen are connected at this point, for the enlargement of mind is required for a life within which actions rest on reflective judgment[34] rather than habit or tradition. When action is based on tradition, habit, the established rule of bureaucracy, or mere determinative judgment, politics and the modern mind ends. As it does so the twin prisons of subjection and subjectivity come to decisive domination. The practical effects are seen clearly in the so-called 'politics' of the *ethnos.* When *ethnos* drives out *demos* closure is sought, alterity expelled, reflective judgment eliminated. By contrast a genuine *demos* is open-textured both to actions and to the future.

The enlargement of the mind and the breakout from subjection and subjectivity cannot be achieved in social or political isolation. There are theoretical grounds for thinking the mind capable of the transformation but there are also grounds for thinking that it also requires the openness of *demos* that is precluded by the structural limitations on full citizenship as that occurs in statist models of government. In turn that cannot be achieved outside the recovery of the political. Taken together the recovery of the political and the further enlargement of the modern mind does invoke the possibility of a citizen self.

4

The Recovery of the Political and the Project of the World

While it is frequently thought that politics is found everywhere and at all times, there is an opposing view that politics ended with the *polis*, which was its context,[1] and that after Machiavelli the prime focus of politics and political theory is centred on statecraft.[2] What is at issue here are two quite different conceptions of politics. In one the focus is on the activity for which the *polis* provided the context; in the other the focus became the abstract object, the state, and how to manage it. On this view what now passes for politics is the management of the modern state. The implication of connecting politics and state in this way is to de-politicise those whose actions fall out of the domain of the state. After Machiavelli modern politics has become increasingly statist in a number of crucial ways, primary among which are that the boundaries of politics are the boundaries of the state and the remit of the state runs to what are described as public affairs. Consequently politics is limited to an agenda set by the state, for it is the state that defines its own boundaries and defines what counts and what does not count as politics. This definition is, of course, all important: whoever defines the boundaries of legitimate state activity sets the political agenda, and whoever defines that sets the limits of citizenship and civic activity. The boundaries are, therefore, not a matter of passing concern; they are a matter of central concern.

The view that politics has been lost, is valuable, and, by implication, requires recovery depends on understanding politics as an activity prior to and more fundamental to statecraft. Statecraft is that activity developed from Machiavelli and which separated people from the immediacy of involvement in the management of their shared affairs. On this view politics is prior to and required for statecraft but it does not follow that statecraft is the satisfactory completion of politics. There is every reason why politics can, and in a political society does, extend beyond the boundaries of the state and it is open to any society or community to seek to foster that extension; to take it as part of its ideals rather than to limit or seek to limit it. Relatedly, of course, citizenship, if that is understood as the description of the status and activity of political people, can apply to domains, areas, activities and actions that are not directly or immediately 'statist'. Taken at its widest, politics is a certain sort of world engagement which, as that contingently developed, produced the state. It does not follow from that that the state is either a necessary consequence of politics or that it is required for politics. On the contrary there is a perfectly defensible view that the state inhibits politics and distorts citizenship. Taken further such an argument implies that there is an activity of politics and citizenship to be found in areas either not bounded by the state or even in an area beyond the state. Such a possibility is enhanced, perhaps even made realisable, as a consequence of, among other things, the end of history. For the end of history in the sense of, first, the end of meta-narratives and, second, the commencement of multiple histories has produced conditions in which there are a variety of voices clamouring for attention. Those voices create spaces within which the political taken as the activity of world engagement and world-making can emerge. When politics is so understood its traditional components are combined with its radical possibilities.

Of Actions and Moments

The phrase, 'the political', seems to have originated with Carl Schmitt in 1932, but the modern form of the nominalisation behind it can be traced back certainly to Otto's phrase, 'The Idea of the Holy', and even to prior nominalisations of which 'The Good' is a paradigmatic example. Such a phrase has a long lineage but in its Kantian form as the contrast between *the right* and *the good* it has entered contemporary debate as the formula that, on some accounts,[3] has come to define liberalism. A phrase like 'the idea of the holy' seems to point to something more enduring than the mere momentary activity of being holy. The holy is good for all time, or for a significant period of time. That the holy could be temporary seems to contain a conflict of ideas. Yet that which is political is normally regarded as transient, not enduring and certainly not eternal; nothing, it seems, is more transitory than politics.[4]

Such a view is both correct and incorrect. Nothing, it might seem, is more transitory than politics as a particular activity, but *the political* is a deeper dimension of life and a deeper human possibility on which it is possible to draw and in which it is possible to participate. That participation is never simple for it is tied in with, and engages with, a cross-section of political, ethical and theological moments each of which, when properly enacted and re-enacted, create and re-create themselves.

In this sense 'the political' is distinguished from politics in that it refers, paradoxically perhaps, to something enduring rather than to something transitory: to that in which one might participate but in which one is not bound to, or obliged to, participate. There is a related distinction that is sometimes made between *la politique* and *le politique*,[5] between what is transitory and a matter of collective day-to-day arrangements and that which transcends those mere day-to-day arrangements. Any society might make some sort of political, and all societies must make some sort of governmental arrangement[6] whereby its affairs are ordered and its continuity ensured.[7] Those arrangements must include the day-to-day management of its affairs. These are the trivia of life which can be found at every level from government down to the minutiae of the household affairs of individuals. Such trivia are indispensable to the cyclical activity of human life, for without them the most basic foundation of that life would be diminished even to vanishing under its own incompetence and its own inability to continue.

At one level they are trivia but looked at from another perspective they may appear as matters of prime importance, for what Oakeshott called 'attending to affairs'[8] is necessary to social and political continuity. Oakeshott's point is significant as is a prior but related point made by Burke.[9] But attending to affairs in this sense is not always by itself an indicator of, or the best practice of, *noblesse humanitas,* and at worst such a view of politics can turn out to be little more than crisis management or mere 'disjointed incrementalism'.[10] Attending to trivia is rarely the stuff of *humanitas* at its best. Taken at its noblest the ideal of *humanitas* includes doing that which people are uniquely fitted to do, not what they are necessarily required to do. It might be objected that such a model of *humanitas* implies some sort of false essentialism; an essentialism that incorporated some particular cultural model and which universalised it, turning it from a noble goal into little more than ideology. This is the basis of Heidegger's critique of humanism, that it incorporates the values of Roman manners and civility while excluding alternatives as barbarous. A similar critique might be applied to taking the political as more than attending to the immediacy of particular affairs in particular places. To take it as more than that, to take it as having some enduring or lasting quality attached to, or incorporated in it, that stretches beyond such mere immediacies might turn out to be no more than taking one limited model and applying it universally. In such a case the search for some wider value would become little more than yet another exercise in ideology. To take the political as identified in some way with an unreconstructed *humanitas* is to fall into the trap of reading one set of cultural values as values for the world and closing out the rather late commencement of multiple histories and multiple voices clamouring for attention.

The issue is whether particular and culturally-specific conceptions of humanity are ineradically wedded to conceptions of the political. Clearly they are related in some sense, for politics as a value is historically related to humanity as a value and that is part of the Western story. The social originary that came to abhor and then to value humanity was presented to the Western mind(s), and I use the term(s) advisedly and with caution, and well represented in the mediated story of the Fall from grace. The account, as given in Genesis, was interpreted by St Paul and then by St Augustine. In miniature all the characteristics, and characters, that are at the foundation of humanism are presented here, first as abhorrence and then as celebration. In a traditional Christian framework there has been a tendency to abhor them. The humanist framework, as it developed not so much from Roman manners but from the rediscovery of Aristotle's *Politics*, inverted the traditional Christian view and came to celebrate politics. The turning point is found first in William of Moerbecke's translation of Aristotle's *Politics*. What William rendered as the term *polistheuma* presented, or rather re-presented to the world, a conception of politics as a worthy rather than an unworthy activity. Dante, in distinguishing secular and sacral powers, extended William's concept of *polistheuma*. He turned it into the concept of *politizare*, the idea of acting politically in a distinctively human way for the sheer pleasure and enjoyment of acting in that way and for its own sake. In this sense politics was not a means–end relation; not a part of some calculus as Machiavelli was to make it; not a statal form as it developed in Europe; but an activity in its own right that was valued and valuable. It celebrated the best of what it was to be distinctively human.

The break from what had preceded it was immense. Prior to Dante politics had been at best an evil necessity forced upon 'man' by virtue of the expulsion from the paradisical condition and the necessities that followed from living in a Fallen state. Dante turned this entire model on its head. The moment of expulsion which the Christian meta-narrative had made definitive of the human condition became a moment not of regret but of celebration. And at its centre was willing, acting, being political and enjoying that activity and condition for its own sake; for being distinctively human. *Politizare* in Dante's terms overturned a sacral tradition which, for the previous millennia following Augustine's, had eliminated will. For now individual will was, as Descartes put it, placed as the greatest of contentments.

The basis of this celebration is clear, bold and compelling. Prior to the breaking of the prime interdict, Adam was not fully human in the sense that he was not mortal, felt no pain and was subject to no ills. Neither was he reflective. When he broke the prime interdict he became human in that he became mortal, felt pain, was subject to ills and became reflective and self-conscious. 'You have become like one of us' was Jahweh's plaint. One can regret that, as a fall from grace, or one can celebrate it as the advent of that which is human. If the latter course is taken then the characters of freedom, will, and individuality become central and can be collectively exercised only through that political tradition which permits the development and action of that which is distinctively human. This requires and may even celebrate the ordering of human affairs by secular and not by sacral means. The final expression of that is the development of that which is the political.

If there is a sacral domain incorporating that which is holy then it is not stretching a point too much to expect that there is a secular domain capturing that which is political. The claims of Schmitt about 'the political' and the claims of Otto about 'the holy' arise out of that cleavage which appeared in the thirteenth century. The roots of the cleavage are found quite clearly in that part of the social originary presented in the mytho-poesis that encapsulates the idea of the Fall. It is in the combination of the image of the Fall and the Church–State split of the thirteenth century that the modern conception of politics as a distinctively human and distinctively joyous activity occurred.

The image of the Fall captures the consequence of an act of human willing. It is willing that is the downfall of Adam. As Adam represents all humanity, so his downfall is the downfall of humanity. This tragedy is, however, when looked at from another prespective, the foundation of humankind, for it is (within the terms of that meta-narrative) willing that is definitive of what it is to be human. The immortal and paradisical life of Adam and Eve which was lived without suffering was not a recognisably human life. It was the expulsion from paradise that brought about the human condition and it was an act of will that led to that expulsion.

Dante and then Descartes turned this wilful moment to political and human effect. Dante turned willing into a human and a joyful moment. In a significant sense willing became definitive of humanity.

That sense of willing and of acting politically as a joy or contentment – *politizare* was an ideal which continued until the rise of the state substituted statecraft for *politizare*. The emergence of the state paralleled the emergence of human individuals, who could obtain, experience, practice and enhance the value of *politizare*. Yet as they emerged, so simultaneously and ironically the rise of statecraft removed the possibility of *politizare* from these newly emergent individuals.

The background which produced conceptions of politics, humanity and their specific relation has developed from the Western tradition and it originary. To that extent, any claim for its wider value would seem to require some kind of additional support to show that the implications of the Western originary and its development had a universal significance. It is unlikely that any such argument or support could be provided. Therefore, it would seem that Western conceptions of politics and humanity are not properly exportable to other cultures. A wider issue is whether that tradition prescribes or forces determinate content or action on another culture. If it does, then it is of course particularistic, and conceptions of both politics and humanity would be merely Western and particularistic. If it does not determine content, then the humanism so construed meets the requirement of a post-humanist humanism which, as Heidegger points out, might, for want of a better label, still be called 'humanism'.

There is a fundamental mistake that lies at the heart of traditional objections to essentialism. It is frequently assumed that a general concept is determined by and, in turn, determines a particular content. A clear example is the argument that Western history represents world history. It is contained, for instance, in Fukayama's argument for liberal triumphalism, but also in Hegel and in some of Marx's account of history. Thus, a particular conception determines a general conception and the general account of history will determine all particular histories.

All such arguments have the same general form: namely 'x' contains 'y' and 'y' is necessary for the satisfactory completion of 'x'. To use a well-worn example: an acorn *must* grow into an oak tree if it is to develop fully, or, within an eschatological framework, the world *must* end in a particular way and people *must* be judged in a particular way at the end of time if the story contained within that meta-narrative is to end in the way determined at its outset.

This general account appears as mistaken once the general structure on which it rests appears as a meta-narrative that lacks credulity. Incredulity might be the basis of an objection that destroyed all essentialist or neo-essentialist formulations. This seems to me to be mistaken. Related and acceptable formulations that avoid the problems given by traditional essentialist formulations are possible. So, for example, to say that someone is uniquely fitted to do something or perform some act is not to imply that they *must* do that thing and that they *must* realise themselves in only that particular way. It is not to say that the realisation of that someone depends only on one outcome and that such an outcome is contained as a necessary outcome of some earlier condition. But it is perfectly reasonable to claim that people must do that which they are uniquely fitted to do, or that a particular person must do that which they are uniquely fitted to do if their potential talents and possibilities are to be realised: this is part of the condition of self-realisation and autonomy. However, it does not follow from the claim that people are fitted to do one thing, or a variety of things, that they are determined to do only one thing and/or that their life must work out in a particular way if it is to be realised. They may be uniquely fitted to do a wide range of things, they may lead a wide range of possible lives and realise themselves in a variety of possible ways: people lead open-textured rather than closed lives, but it does not follow from that open-texturedness that the language of self-realisation is meaningless.

Traditional essentialism understands realisation to be identical to only one end point or *telos*. By contrast, what is argued here is that there may be an undetermined and undeterminable number and variety of possible realisations, any of which would satisfy a condition of realisation, and none of which are teleologically, historically, or otherwise determined as an outcome. They may or may not come about. We understand this well when we note that there are a variety of paths down which a life might travel and not realise or not fully realise itself. We recognise this when we say that someone wasted their life, or that they wasted their talent, or that they wasted their potential. Such claims do not invoke some underlying eschatological-teleological model against which the success or failure of a particular life is judged. It is rather that the range of talents of particular individuals is recognised, and a judgment is made as to whether or not those talents were fully realised. There is nothing fixed or determinate in such claims. On the contrary the open-endedness of such lives is recognised, admitted and affirmed. Thus to say someone did not realise their potential is to say, or imply, that of the range of things that they might have done, of the range of potentials that they might have developed, they failed to achieve the one noted.

This argument denies eschatological essentialism, while permitting personal autonomy, individual self-determination, politics as *politizare* and a conception of humanity as an enlarged form of humanism. To take and draw upon the concept of the political as a personal activity is always to engage in a personal statement: a statement that may be open to revision but which also always contains within it the possibility of taking a stand, of drawing a line, of saying, with Luther, 'Here I stand, I can no more' – or of saying, to take and modify an argument from Rorty, 'This is my final discourse. I can explain it no further.' Of course to take that stand and to draw that line is to move beyond the 'final discourse' to the value of self-determination and to engagement with 'the political' at its deepest. A claim that I can explain myself, or we can explain ourselves, no further implies also that I, or we, feel the need for explanation has gone far enough and the point of self-assertion has been reached. That self-assertion or self-determination is the point of autonomy when it is primarily individual and the point of the political when it is primarily shared or agonistic. The connection between the pure moment of the political and the pure moment of the holy is evident in those great moments when they are found together in one person in one act.

What is said of individual self-determination can be said of cultural and political self-determination. So a culture or a political community might adopt a final discourse but in so doing it is resting that final discourse on a more fundamental value of self-determination, willing, sharing in the operation of its own collective life and so on. To assert that one has a final discourse that is not negotiable is already to appeal to values prior to that final discourse, values that are negotiable and that rest on something not unrelated to the values found in Dante's *politizare*, and in *humanitas* understood in that wider sense.

Similarly, to say that *humanitas* is doing that which it is uniquely fitted to do is not to travel down some Aristotelian, or eschatological, or teleological, or other deterministic path. It is to say instead that there are a variety of paths down which a life might travel and realise itself. There is nothing deterministic, teleological, or inescapably Eurocentric about that kind of observation. To be in charge of one's own life does not determine any particular content or any particular form of that charge. To be engaged in and to accept the value of *politizare* does not imply enjoying the value of *politizare* in any particular way. To accept this as a part of the human condition, of being human or of *humanitas* does not determine any particular content or, by implication, any particular cultural preference. It views willing, participating, sharing in the operation of one's own life as a value but it does not say that it must be exhibited in any particular way or that it must be done in any particular way or that it must contain any particular content. It provides a formula or map within which such elements can be contained but it does not follow from such a map that any particular content is specified.

Of course there is not and never can be a completely neutral map. Being political, willing, judging, sharing in the operation of one's own life and sharing in the conditions of that operation are valued conceptions. But they are not entirely optional values, for in a world at the commencement of histories, where there are a variety of voices, there is no alternative to being political, willing, judging and sharing the dimensions of life in some way. A map, or at least a matrix that includes those components or something equivalent to those components, which accepts that while different people have final discourses those final discourses rest on values that all appeals to final discourses share, permits a reconstructed *humanitas*, and given that some starting place is required this is neither bad nor without its attractions.

Actions and Contexts

Some of the greatest political moments have also been great religious moments. So Luther and Gandhi brought changes to an entire age not merely by challenging an entire orthodoxy or by challenging it in unusual ways but by challenging it in ways that, first, crossed acceptable boundaries of interpretation and, second, by incorporating in themselves the political and the holy at its deepest and most fundamental level. In doing that they challenged the sacral–secular distinction not in some trivial or minor way but in a way that exhibited their full participation in domains that are generally regarded as incapable of co-existence. The political and the holy were present in both cases.

That such instances are both startling and startlingly clear arises from the strong distinction drawn between different types of action. There is a deep tradition of distinguishing between political and religious action and, since Machiavelli, but also to some extent since St Augustine of Hippo, a strong tradition of distinguishing between political and ethical action. At its most extreme, politics, by which is generally meant the state, acts according to its own imperatives and is excluded from normal ethical concerns. That this realism is both possible and frequently seen as necessary is due to a series of ruptures in the world that tore the ethico-political moment apart. In consequence to act politically is frequently regarded as acting against ethical precepts or as acting with disregard for ethics.

The rift expressed by Machiavelli, and afterwards by a long line of so-called realist writers, has pointed up the consequences of the structural changes and ruptures that brought the modern world into being. After Machiavelli political realism was, and to some extent still is, the dominant mode of understanding the actions of states and of state actors.

There is another and more subtle expression of the rupture, however, and it lies in David Hume's distinction between observations of fact and observations of norm or value. Hume observes how writers frequently slide from observation of what is the case to what ought to be the case with little or no pause. This, he claims, is an illegitimate move for it conflates questions of what is the case with questions of what ought to be the case. Hume's fork, as it has come to be known, sits well with Machiavelli's guillotine, as I shall call it. Both slice or separate into different domains, components or parts that which has not always been in separate domains, components or parts. Both have done this with such clarity, conviction and success that the separation comes to appear as natural.

The logical basis of both Machiavelli's guillotine and Hume's fork is to distinguish between different sorts of action on the basis of the manner of the individuation of an action. So, if an action is political, certain rules apply to it; if it is ethical, different rules apply. If it is factual, it comes under one set of headings; if normative under another. What is ultimately at issue is the means by which an action is individuated and classified. To take an extreme but telling case, Adolph Eichmann did not, on his own account, participate in the killing of Jews in the Holocaust because as a bureaucrat and administrator he merely, as he put it, 'sat at my desk and did my business'.[11]

This argument may seem facile but it goes to the issue of what counts as an event. An occurrence, having a clear temporal beginning and end, is inadequate as a criterion, appealing though it may be at first sight. A clap of thunder might seem to be an event, but why? Because it has a determinate beginning and end perhaps. But if that is the criterion then almost anything will count as an event. As Broad once put it, 'the white cliffs of Dover are a long boring event'.[12] By contrast what seem to be determinate events can be broken up, so, as Davidson put it, a claim that the shark ate Johnny can be broken up into the shark ate Johnny's leg, the shark ate Johnny's foot, the shark ate Johnny's ..., and so on.[13]

These examples show among other things that events in themselves are difficult to individuate and that it is difficult to individuate events as being of a certain sort, as, for instance, political events or social events. Such difficulties seem to play into the hands of Eichmann for they appear to make it difficult to challenge his claim that he merely 'sat at his desk and did his business'.

Such a description of actions depends on morally separating or distancing an action from its effects. It is far from clear that it is defensible either in particular cases like that of Eichmann or in general. If it is not defensible it is because actions are never completely isolated or 'distant' one from another or from wider effects. And if actions are not so isolatable or distant, then politics and ethics are similarly not so isolatable. There are numerous consequences of this but one would be that citizenship is not merely a matter of actions relating to some statist conception of politics but a matter of actions relating to wider conceptions of politics. A second would be that such actions cannot be divorced from the ethical domain – they are either also a part of the ethical domain or are related to it. A further consequence of this is to relate the moment of politics contained in the idea of the political and the moment of ethics. This rapprochement takes place in what I will call the act-moment and it has a modern and a classical dimension.

The modern dimension arises as a consequence of taking actions or event actions as part of a wider social matrix. An action can be variously understood as either behaviour with attached intention,[14] as in the analytic tradition, as behaviour that is meaningful, as in the sociological tradition stemming from Weber[15] and then Alfred Schutz,[16] or it may be understood as revelation through speech in the 'space of appearances', as in Arendt.[17] The latter is slightly idiosyncratic and resists further analytic analysis if only because it is given as a primitive within the argument. It also breaks so completely with all other contemporary uses of the term action that it can be set aside for the moment.[18]

That leaves a need to further analyse action as either intended behaviour or as meaningful behaviour. Allegedly there is a difference between these two models. The force of the idea of intended behaviour can, on the face of it, be individualistic whereas the force of the idea of meaningful behaviour cannot. Ultimately the difference may be more apparent than real. Take, for instance, an example offered by Max Weber.[19] Weber argued that the centre of an action subsisted with the individual. Thus to make sense of what someone in a forest chopping wood was doing we needed to know the intention they attached to the action. They might, for instance, be working off a fit of rage, they might be a woodcutter cutting wood or a variety of other possibilities. This places the source of the action, what it is and how it is to be described with the individual. This individualistic conception of action was exploded by Alfred Schutz who showed that any form of meaning had to take place within a social matrix. Meaning is intersubjective. A woodcutter, for instance, was a woodcutter only against a social background within which the activity and the occupation of being a woodcutter cutting wood made sense.[20] The upshot of this is that what appears as even individualistic behaviour is not merely individual; it is part of a social matrix.

What this implies is that an action that is treated as behaviour with an attached intention, or treated as behaviour that is meaningful, can be completely understood only when the appropriate matrix is supplied and known. What it further implies is that a political action cannot be defined as a political action independently of the intention and/or meaning attached to it. This can be taken further and seems to imply that the treatment of a mere event as such does not allow the event to be individuated as a particular kind of event without further information. To put this another way, an event cannot be said to be a political event, a social event, a musical event, a sporting event and so on without the relevant social, intentional and/or meaning matrix into which it fits and in which it subsists. Any action and, more broadly, any life requires some hermeneutic backdrop against which it interprets its actions and in which it provides its particular and general meanings. That backdrop might be readily accepted or it might not be so easily accepted; it might well be something against which it rails and against which it fights, as Prometheus, Antigone, Socrates, Jesus, Luther, Gandhi, Mandela found themselves doing in different ways but to similar effect.

The determination of that which counts as a political action while simultaneously extending beyond the confines of politics narrowly understood depends on both the backdrop and the conception of action offered. From Machiavelli and Hume these are generally taken as distinct, but as I have shown, they are distinctions not beyond contemporary challenge. That contemporary challenge seeks to undercut Machiavelli's guillotine and Hume's fork. But there is a classic source to the problem of which it could be said that both Machiavelli and Hume are merely the inheritors. The social originary of that source is well focused in the expulsion of the poets from the Republic, and in the war between poetry and philosophy that followed and which was embedded in the political thought of the next two and a half millennia.

In *The Republic* III Plato denies a poet entry to the city on the grounds that such a man could assume any shape and bring about any transformation. The poet through his imagery can undercut and undermine the truth and order which it is the purpose of the Republic to represent and incorporate. It is this moment that is the defining separation between philosophy and poetry, a moment that has led to a war between them which has come to be central to and characteristic of their relation during the following two and a half millennia. That war is significant, for in separating concerns of philosophy from concerns of poetry it has privileged the idea of objective truth over matters of interpretation. It is interpretation that Plato wished to be banished from the Republic and the poet could do that for he was 'capable by his cunning of assuming every kind of shape and imitating all things'.[21]

This connection is significant and the ignorance of its effects is significant for it fosters, even requires, a false distinction between action and politics that is little more than a continuance of the false war between poetry and philosophy begun by Plato and one which requires overcoming if a deeper conception of action, politics and citizenship is to be recovered.

The contextualised model of action provided in Schutz's critique of Weber begins the rapprochement for it places actions and event acts in a social context and a social matrix. Understood more widely, that social matrix is not a map incorporating some objective truth – it is rather a matrix incorporating some understandings of the way in which a particular society and culture relates things. Eichmann was wrong because he broke that understanding and he broke any reasonable construction that could be placed on that understanding.

Such constructions, comprehension and understandings are always related to the narratives we tell ourselves and each other about ourselves and about the world in which we live. Such stories as narratives and as poetry provide a context within which the particularity of actions make sense. But they make sense not as action in some purely formal and ahistorical sense, but as action set against a narrative backdrop. They make sense as action in context but both the action and the context taken separately and, more significantly, together are always partly poetic. But it does not follow from the observation that our narratives and stories are poetic that we have some strangely unlimited poetic licence to cause every kind of rift and rupture that it is theoretically possible to bring about. Every culture contains tensions that might be exploited but it does not follow that there is an obligation to so exploit them. To take that road is to follow a set of values that would need justifying in extra-cultural terms. Such terms would have to invoke some degree of objectivity and would therefore be self-defeating of the original nihilist tendency. There is no systematically arguable case for such nihilism and there is no systematically arguable case for wanton cultural destruction as opposed to reasoned cultural critique. Two and a half millennia on, there is a good case for admitting the poets back into the Republic – there was not then and is not now a case for admitting the cultural thug.

What this admission implies is that the sharp distinction drawn between philosophy and poetry from Plato onwards and which is found in politics in Machiavelli's wretched guillotine, and in philosophy in Hume's ideologically contaminated fork, can be potentially ameliorated if not completely overcome. The gap that is thrown up in either of these cases cannot be completely eliminated, for in a dynamic world it is always possible to offer accounts of what ought to be the case, and it is not possible in such a world to determine with finality what counts as either an act or an act-event or an event or an act-event of a particular kind. An event is not naturally a political event or an act a political event in its own right. It cannot be individuated as a political event by virtue of some inherent or intrinsic characteristic. What makes it a political or social or ethical or other event is because it is interpreted as such; it becomes so by convention or by construction and interpretation in the minds of those who regard it.

The political implications of this include that what counts as a political event is the political construction that is put upon the event, and that what counts as a political act is the political construction that is put upon the act itself.[22] When this argument is taken to its limit it seems that what counts as politics is itself a political issue *par excellence*. And what goes into what counts as politics includes the story, narrative or poetic backdrop against which events and acts are determined as political event or acts.

One way of setting the political agenda for the world is, therefore, as Augustine, Kant, Hegel, Marx and Fukayama have done, to attempt to write world history as Western history. This stifles alternative voices by discounting them as genuine political voices and turning them into social, cultural or private noises of a temporary kind, a kind that will eventually succumb to the *Parousia*, *Moralität*,

Sittlichkeit, Communism or Liberal triumphalism as the case may be.

Turned around, a political act subsists within a narrative and poetic background. A political act cannot be separated from its poetic context; a political act is, therefore, not an act that continues the war between philosophy and poetry; but is one that brings the tensions of that war into itself. A truly political act, an act that recovers the political, is not divisive in the Machiavellian sense or logically destructive in the Humean sense. It contains rather a creative tension in a pre-Platonic, or even in a contemporary and post-Platonic sense: in that condition where the poets are admitted back into the Republic.

A political act is neither an act without poetry or poetry without an act; it is an act-moment. It reconciles the abstraction of the act-event with the poetic backdrop within which it takes place. It implies that the narrative structure of a society provides the context within which actions make sense. Such a structure rules out divisive constructions of acts and returns poetry to the domain of action. The act-moment cannot be realised within the confines of the state as traditionally understood. That has been, and is, too confining, too divisive and too forgiving of that kind of moral distance that has produced a raft of related actions ranging from Pontius Pilate to Adolph Eichmann.

This moral distance is appealing. It draws one away from the wider consequences of one's own acts and permits a narrow conception of self and world within which one resides. It is also dangerous for it permits the avoidance of wider responsibilities and wider conceptions and perceptions of the world. A wider conception of self and world is one in which deeper components are participated, thus the political, the good and the holy provide the possibility of recovering the ethico-political moment in a significant way. There are several levels at which this might be understood, but at its clearest it means little more than bringing poetry and poetic understanding back into life and accepting that actions extend beyond their immediate confines and that Machiavelli's guillotine and Hume's fork have in that confluence of the political, the holy and the good which emerges as the act-moment eased their hold. Such an easing of the hold of the guillotine and the fork is to begin also the break from the trap that the modern conception of politics forces upon us.

To break from that trap is to begin the recovery of the political, a recovery that requires reconstruing politics in terms that shift away from the event/statist paradigm conception of politics. It means among other things that the recovery of the political is tied into that larger project of the recovery of the world. Such an activity steps away from limited conceptions and perceptions of action and engages with its wider contexts. That context can be understood only by bringing the recovery of the political together with its pre-Platonic roots in *poesis*. Another way of putting this is that the recovery of the political requires relating philosophy, poetry and action. Looked at from another aspect, the twin impossibilities of either completely describing the world in terms of the claimed truth of philosophical terms or of rendering it completely into poetry, of poeticising the world, result in tensions that between them permit, even force, the appearance and continuance of politics. Philosophy and poetics may make strange, sometimes uncomfortable and sometimes quarrelsome bedfellows but bedfellows they must be if politics is to emerge.

The Project of the World

The narrative and poetic components in politics draw attention to a distinction that can be, yet rarely is, drawn between a world project and the project of the world. When Nietzsche argued that 'hitherto there have been a thousand goals', he also went on to argue that 'the goal for humanity is humanity itself'.[23] What is at issue is whether that goal is to be humanity in the narrow sense so rightly criticised by Heidegger, or in the broader and reconstructed sense that I offered in the previous section.

A world project takes one narrative or poetic perspective and legislates that perspective as the only valid perspective. In its minimalist form it can be relatively harmless, appealing to and legislating only to the already persuaded. So Plato's *Republic* legislated for that city, while More's *Utopia* legislated for the members of that utopia. In more recent guise such models recur as communes, or as religious cults, of varying kinds that seek little more than the right to live out their life in the way they choose. There is a sense in which such communities do no more than any other community that claims and seeks autonomy and self-determination: they look to live out their life in their own way and within limits which in general terms at least are not difficult to specify. There seems little objection in principle to such a desire. Indeed it may even be a fundamental desire of peoples and a fundamental necessity to have a mode of life that they can call their own and that has some degree of self-determination in it. The qualifier 'some degree of self-determination' is clearly necessary, for with a few vanishing exceptions all forms of life impinge on other forms of life.

Forms of life that are autonomous or relatively autonomous can be regarded as 'worlds'. There is a trivial and a serious sense to that designation. They are worlds in that their members share assumptions that determine the edges, boundaries or cut-off points of their 'world' and share, therefore, a conception of what is contained within that world. The more serious sense arises from the observation that sets of shared assumptions, language, turns of phrase, concepts, horizons, boundaries, inclusions and exclusions, create an outlook, paradigm, *Weltanschauungen* or other perspective that produces a holistically self-contained perspective. Such an outlook then becomes not so much a mere perspective on the world in which they live as definitive of the world in which they live.

This is a potential point of conflict with other possibly incompatible and self-contained perspectives, and it is a potential source of hegemony: the imposition of one view of the world on others who do not share that view. At its most extreme it attempts to impose that one view on the rest of the world. The general form of that mechanism is to insist that the world view offered is not parochial and particular but expansive and universal. It contains a truth to which others ought and may be forced to conform. In a peculiar inversion of Hume's fork, the maxim that 'is does not imply ought', it turns out that 'ought' requires 'is'.

In such a hegemonic case the relation between poetry and politics resurfaces as the return of the meta-narrative. There are numerous examples: the account of the Hebraic peoples as the chosen peoples; the *Parousia* of St Paul; the Apostles and Augustine; and the linearity in history implied by the belief in the Second Coming as the kingdom of God on Earth; Kant's *Moralität*; Hegel's *Sittlichkeit*; Marx's Communism; Hitler's *Volk* and the Third Reich; Fukayama's liberal triumphalism; and related models of the ideal political and/or ethical order. All subsume other histories and other cultures into and under themselves. In all these examples the history and outlook of one people is provided as the history and outlook of all peoples. Perhaps because the source for this is to be found in the Hebraic conception of movement, exodus and return,[24] its most extreme expression is in the *Volkish* perspective of the Third Reich, which necessarily required the destruction of the Jews. They offered a meta-narrative and an account of universality that was at odds with the claims of the Third Reich – only one of these meta-narratives could be true. As the other could not be converted or incorporated so it required annihilation. The ultimate source of the Final Solution was not the distaste or dislike of the Jews. That could have been, and until a particular point had been, accommodated. What could not be accommodated was their meta-narrative. Their poetic story of the world was fundamentally at odds with the claimed truth of the Third Reich. So much so that they could not co-exist.

It is this kind of observation and conflict that lies behind the claim that there have been many world projects. It is also clear that all have been mistaken; they have taken some aspect of the social originary and shifted it from narrative background to all-encompassing truth. In consequence all have carried a model that privileged one way of life. But as yet there has been no serious project of the world. The distinction is important. A world project and a project of the world both take the world as their object, but the means by which they arrive at that object and the nature of the concern is quite different. A world project is hegemonic, absolutist and dictatorial while a project of the world is not. One is *a priori* and imposed while the other is *a posteriori* and yet to be discovered. One is required and is the subject of force, the other is invited and is the subject of political negotiation.

There is a variety of different cultures, each with their own poetry and each with their own narratives within which they explain their place in the world and within which they interpret the world. No one narrative and no one poetic account of the world may predominate. The end of history and the commencement of a variety of distinct and different voices implies a variety of different sounds and voices making different sorts of claims on the world. It does not follow from this that all and any claims are permitted. The cultural thug has no licence and the wantonly destructive no place. As Locke said, the world is not for the quarrelsome and the contentious. The world at its most general can incorporate voices and demands that are supportive of but not destructive of it. A variety of voices are permitted, even encouraged, but to admit and encourage a variety of voices is not to encourage and respect just any noise in the pretence that it is a voice. Nihilism for its own sake, for example, is not a voice, it is merely a noise.

What this implies is that the foundation of the project of the world depends on an *a posteriori* outlook on the ways in which aspects of the world might be related. Some such project is necessary for world appreciation and survival. Such a project requires difference and alterity and has no previously fixed model of institutions, practices or affairs that it seeks to instantiate. All that is required of such a project is that whatever practices are sought, and whatever practices or institutions are established, that they be world enhancing and world promoting. There are numerous and as yet unknown and multiply various ways in which this can be done. The ways of the world are many and the practices and institutions that can be world enhancing are many, varied and pregnant with possibilities. It is possible to proscribe certain activities, certain institutions and certain practices while prescribing nothing beyond the general point that whatever is done should promote and not damage the world and the people in it.

Yet it is also clear that the particularities of cultures, must, except if completely isolated, act towards some conception of the universal. This raises a fundamental issue as to whether different particularities can discover a universal towards which they can act which, while preserving their uniqueness, permits them to share in the world. This implies a limited amount of tolerance towards particularities. Particularity is important but it is not the prime value; indeed taken to its extreme it is self-defeating. If adopted as a prime value it is no more than a return to the hegemonies of the single narrative masquerading as world history. What is wrong with the *Parousia* or with communism or with liberal triumphalism is the expansion of their particularity as universal. Particularity writ large is ideology; imposed on the world it is hegemony; imposed forcefully on the world it is open tyranny. The value of particularity lies in its vulnerability, in not accepting it as a universal, in limiting respect to it as but one voice and in not elevating either that voice or the justification for listening to the voice as if it were a supreme value. To do that would, in the context of one world, ultimately destroy that world, and as it destroyed that world so it would destroy the value of particularity.

If particularity is to be valued, encouraged and permitted it must enhance the world or be at least neutral with respect to the project of the world. At the margins it will frequently be difficult to distinguish between these. It will not generally, however, be difficult to distinguish between those activities that undercut the project of the world and those activities that enhance it. Dumping nuclear waste, for example, is not a contribution to the project of the world and cannot be construed as such no matter how hard the spin-doctors do their spinning. Creating the means by which food can be grown in an otherwise famine-stricken land contributes to the project of the world and that cannot be denied no matter how hard the spin-doctors do their spinning.

The project of the world is a point arrived at *a posteriori* which lies somewhere between the particular and the universal. It seeks to discover the ways in which a variety of narratives can be brought together in a way that requires of each of them a reach towards the common, of an act into the universal. Such a project is creative in a fundamental sense. When the cities of Greece and Rome were founded it was as a part of a religious ceremony. It was taken that such an act of creation required the assistance and support of the gods. There is an even more fundamental precursor to that idea: it is in the creation of the gods and then of the cosmos itself.

In the most fundamental mytho-poetic form that peoples give in their social originary they account first for the coming into being of the gods, the theogony, and then the coming into being of the universe, the cosmogony, the way in which the gods made or transformed the world. Politics takes that second foundational moment, the way in which the gods transformed or made the world, the creation of the *cosmos*, and removes that task from the gods and places it with people. Politics, in that sense, is world-making.[25]

Sharing in the project of the world as world-making is a political activity at any time but world-making against the backdrop of a variety of voices and a variety of narratives is the political task of our times. It is a task that is halted when an effective and closed social originary denies to people a significant place in fashioning the world. That closure and that denial occur whenever the narrative or originary of a people turns into the narrative and the *telos* of the peoples of the world. It closes their openness and silences the voices of others. It matters not what the particular story of the meta-narrative might be, communism, liberalism or whatever – all have the same effect of closure and tyranny.

To turn away from closure and towards the openness involved in the project of the world, a world that is to be discovered as a matter of shared enterprise, is to participate in that kind of creation that is characteristic of the holy, as that is mytho-poetically understood, while also participating in the political and engaging in the ethical. These dimensions and roads to open political action cannot be entirely separated without repeating the rupture expressed in Machiavelli's guillotine and in Hume's fork.

A more positive and forward-looking alternative is to invoke 'the political' as a poetic act moment which intersects with creation and with ethics. At the point of the political the engagement and re-engagement in the world is discovered, enacted and re-enacted. In such circumstances an act becomes for the world and not merely for the self. 'The political' is the moment of the rediscovery, engagement in and the re-creation of the wholeness of human action and activity. It is a moment both temporally and poetically. It is a moment temporally for the point of action and decision is temporal. But that point contains within it the *poesis* and the *mytho-poesis* of an entire tradition. It stretches back to its known origins in the mirror that is the social originary and in which the cosmos was brought into being.

The political brings with it what Descartes referred to, when he describes willing, as 'the greatest contentment', and projects Dante's *humanitas* into a world that has yet to see the proper and full re-alisation of an *a posteriori* humanism: a humanism arising out of experience rather than a humanism imposed on experience. The recovery of and the participation of the political depends upon sharing in the project of the world. Such an activity brings its own problems with it. She or he who engages in the project of the world is always alone in the singularity of the act-moments in which they engage. Decisions and act-moments are always one's own alone but they are also and always made for and in the world which they are always creating and re-creating. This is the condition to which we are condemned, and for which there is no algorithmic solution to be found. It is the condition of radical democracy, deep citizenship and serious engagement with the world.

There are a variety of ways in which that condition and engagement can be expressed. A fundamental sense is to place it as that condition between the universal and the particular. This is best expressed by Plato as *metaxy*, or in-betweenness, the most basic form of which is to be between here and eternity.[26] *Metaxy* is the condition that provides the tensions within which the problems of life, politics and being arise. It is also the foundation on which politics can arise. Politics is a certain sort of world engagement and world-creation, for the activity of politics takes what it finds and, in its world engagement, transforms that world.

The recovery of the political, a task impossible until recently, is now possible against a backdrop in which a single world history and a single meta-narrative has collapsed. The consequence of that collapse is the emergence of a variety of voices that frequently pull in different directions. That diversity can be respected but not endlessly indulged, for there are some aspects of the world that we must share. This implies a project of the world in which care of that world is centre stage but where the precise nature and content of that care is an outcome of discovery and not yet another *a priori*, hegemonic and tyrannical voice.

The recovery of the political is possible against a backdrop in which the project of the world has emerged as a project in which shared participation is possible and in which an *a posteriori* outcome is feasible. The original context of politics ended with the *polis* and was neither fully re-created nor can be re-created in its original manner; but it does recur and always in that point of decision that lies between philosophy and poetry, between the particular and the universal and in the actual activity abandoned by the gods and now belonging to the post-humanistic humanity of shared world-making.

5

Between the Public and the Private

The political contains activity and poetry in an irreducible and potentially healthy tension: a tension which while varying in content from
time to time and place to place goes right to the foundation of the
tradition. Founding moments do determine the range of possible
future stories but they do not determine the stories themselves: that
would imply either that the end of the story was contained in its
beginning or that the content of the story itself lay at some point
outside the story. Either of those perspectives would invoke an
Aristotelian, Augustinian, Marxist or liberal triumphalist account
of history. The first lines in a narrative provide a foundation for
the rest of the narrative but they do not determine the actual
content or even the particular direction that the rest of the narrative
will take. It is the subsequent poets, narrators and actors that work
on and modify what they find as a given.

The narrative from which politics sprang contained at least two
opposing possibilities in it. The first took politics and citizenship
as merely an aspect of life, the second took politics and citizenship
as central to life. The distinction is of major significance, for in one,
citizenship is merely an addition to life, while in the other, citizenship,
understood as the political mode of being, is of such significance
that it is definitive of what it is to be distinctively human. There is
no point in history and society in which either of these models have
completely prevailed. Rather, there are points in history, society
and philosophy when they have varied in their emphasis. Dante or
Arendt, for example, have placed acting politically as of greater
import in life than is generally found in classical liberal theory where
the greatest prizes in life are generally understood to take place in
the private domain.

On the whole the modern Western trend has been to distinguish
citizenship from private living and to separate it out as an aspect
of life which places occasional duties on someone while also
providing a formal status. In general this is true of the Greek *polis*,
of the city of Rome, of the revitalisation of the cities in early modern
Europe and in the civic republicanism of Florence of the
Quattrocentro. It received its greatest transformation and support,
however, in those great religious statements from St Paul, Augustine,
Luther, Calvin and later figures that invented and placed privacy

of thought, conscience and communion with God as a prime value. The split between demands that do not arise immediately from the polity and the more immediate demands of the polity is potentially great: it is at the heart of the modern Western tradition of theo-political thought. Nor is it a merely archaic division, for in secularised and individualised form it lies at the root of the distinction between public and private: a distinction which is one of the clearest hallmarks of liberal thought.

However, this distinction does have precursors in an earlier and more basic distinction between the public and the non-public. In that form its roots are clearly marked in the social originary from which it has arisen, a form that has permitted or even demanded that the disenfranchisement of women, the institution of slavery and a thousand other problems go unremarked. They go unremarked either because a political life is exclusive or because a non-political life is regarded as sufficient for most people. These reasons are different but the outcome is similar: it has de-politicised actual living, even to the point of passing off a de-politicised life as a virtue, while also defining virtue in such a way that it can be achieved only in the private domain. This inverted definition of virtue runs very deep and has some persuasive features. It might even be compelling if the world was in a less than critical condition. As it is, individual and personal responsibilities need to reach further than the private domain.

Nonetheless the distinction between the public and the non-public reaches very deeply into the political culture which has grown up in the West. It is a distinction that is deeply sedimented into political life and which even through its various transformations cannot readily be cast aside. It can, however, be modified without loss of some of its more valuable features. This permits the pos-sibility of developing a concept of the citizen which refers to a mode of political being related less to the formality of space or domain, or duties attached to it, than to the manner and mode of the action itself. I will argue that some actions, normally regarded as private actions, are acts of citizenship and that some actions, regarded as public or general, are not acts of citizenship. I will argue that an act of deep citizenship transcends these traditional distinctions. Deep citizenship is concerned less with the domain within which the act takes place than with the trajectory of an act. An act, from whatever domain, public or private, that is oriented to the particular, the private or the sectional is not an act of citizenship. By contrast an act from whatever domain that is oriented towards the universal is an act of deep citizenship.

An implication of this is that an act of citizenship may emerge from what has traditionally been regarded as the private domain. Relatedly, that which has traditionally been taken to be a private act may also turn out to be a political act, not merely because its consequences have political effects but because it falls under reasonable criteria that might be used to individuate an act as this or as that kind of act. The criteria that permit an act to be individuated or described as a particular sort of act are sufficiently ambiguous to also permit or allow the development of the modern self – that kind of self-consciousness that inhabits a moral space and which is reflexively conscious of that habitation. That self-consciousness is both private in its appreciation of the moral space and public in its appreciation of the shared and public responsibilities of such space. Out of that ambiguity arises that ambiguous being, the citizen self. The citizen self, I shall argue, is a model of the self that lives in and arises out of the tensions of Western society. It is a natural outcome of those tensions but one that exhibits the tensions of that society: tensions that permit, among other things, a thoughtful mode of being.

In the Deepest Recesses

Any distinction between human and citizen risks, and often achieves, an ongoing de-politicisation. The category of human is not necessarily regarded or treated as a political category,[1] whereas the category of citizen is necessarily political. So a woman might be regarded as a human but not a citizen and, on some accounts, a slave might be regarded as a human (or part-human) but not a citizen. In both cases while the humanity is permitted it is de-politicised. A paradox of the Western outlook is that it can invent the political outlook while simultaneously building exclusion and de-politicisation into that outlook. Generally the tradition has tended, although not without contestation, to place the public above the private. Thus in the pantheon, in Antigone, in Solon and even in the relation between Adam and God, where Adam was forced to reveal the reason for seeking a space away from God, the private was ultimately taken to be subservient to the public. But the fact that these domains are contestable and that they have been the subject of notable contests is itself a necessary part of the political tradition. In all these cases the contests arise as a consequence of the condition of living between the particular and the universal. This is the *metaxial* condition of Being that lies between the immediate and the eternal.[2]

Some kind of early contest between the public and that which lies outside the public domain can be found in the earliest part of the social originary. So the gods of the Mesopotamian pantheon met in assembly, took decisions in assembly and enacted such decisions as were commanded by the assembly. At the same time it is clear that they had a life independent of the assembly. The general form of that myth shifted in two ways: one was into the experience that was to lead to the Christian tradition and the other was into the Hellenistic tradition. In its Hellenistic form the model led to such weight being placed on the *polis* that the demands and claims of the *polis* were quite frequently expected to override all other loyalties. Antigone's fate, for instance, was sealed partly by her failure to pay sufficient weight to the importance of the *polis* – to the public. There is a not completely unrelated point made by Solon. When he saw the damage that was done to the temples by those raiding their wealth for private gain he pointed out how the perpetrators would suffer and would not be able to escape the public wrath wrought by the gods:

> When evil falls upon public life its scourge invades the private lives of all men. A man who thinks it can be escaped by hiding within the jurisdiction and confines of his own home is not secure, for even his house fails to furnish him with security. Such public evil vaults over the wall of his courtyard, however high that wall might be and finds him out, even should he turn and run and conceal himself in the deepest recesses of his own apartments[3]

This section from the fragment is significant for it makes a clear distinction between the public and the non-public yet shows how the public can 'vault' into the deepest recesses of the household. In all these examples there is a distinction between public and that which lies outside the public but it is one that can be overridden by higher authority.

The importance of the delineation of the public domain is continued by Aristotle, who defined a city as its citizens and a citizen as one who shares in its government;[4] by the Roman Republicans; in the Germanic cities of the thirteenth century; in a variety of humanist revivals; and in civic republicanism in its various guises up to, including and possibly beyond some contemporary communitarian theories. At the same time as the claimed dominance of the public were the growing claims of the private. It is in privacy of conscience, privacy of moral space and privacy of thought that we find the development of that cast of mind which led to individualism. Without that individualism there would be no moral agent distinct from the public domain.

There are two models of politics that may arise from these tensions. First, models, whether ancient or modern, that distinguish between specific political identity consequent on the city and, second, models of politics that exclude any significant life beyond the private. The *locus classicus* of the latter is Hobbes who rejected Aristotle and his premises that man was *zoon politikon* and made it clear that he thought the emerging modern state an artifice.

Man had preceded the state and man by his own art had imitated the, 'Art of God' in his creation of the world.[5]

It followed from the premise of the state as an artifice that man was not, as Aristotle had claimed, *zoon politikon*. He was not a political animal, as such, but political only by dint of his ability to construct a state. 'Man' was a subject and excluded from public affairs. But he was also subject in another sense: he was, by implication, a subject of consciousness. His consciousness was significantly prior to the society of which he was a part, but once the state was established it was then subject to the state. So Hobbes carried his linguistic theory of nominalism to the point where the Leviathan was empowered to provide 'the apt imposition of names', a device that governed individual consciousness.

Yet privacy of consciousness and conscience was sufficiently great that it could be prior to and dangerous to the formation of society itself. That danger arose from the view that autonomous individuals were responsible directly to God for their actions in the world. This potential source of dissent and conflict was, for Hobbes, a source of conflict to be obliterated.

The demands of a private space capable of challenging the public dominance are marked. Exceptions to public dominance are notably, even paradigmatically, exhibited in conscientious objection; a value that was itself consequent on the growth of self, conscience and its religious significance. From Luther, Calvin and right through the Protestant tradition it is the individual that is responsible for their mental space, their conscience and their actions. The significant dimensions of life are, on this view, predominantly private. The public is necessary and obedience to it is generally necessary, but it is not fundamental to life, to living, to mental space, to consciousness and to self-identity. This is a significant and valuable human perception, but it is also one in which the self was conceived in private rather than in public terms and in which the public was conceived in liberal rather than in civic terms.

To conceive of the self in such liberal and juridical terms de-politicises 'humanity'. The effect was noted by Marx. 'Who', he reasonably wanted to know, 'is this man distinct from the citizen?'[6] One is ostensibly a juridical category while the other is not, and bourgeois civil society separated man and citizen where citizenship was most likely to be a term used to signify a bearer of certain status rights with respect to a state. In many European cases the 'citizen' had so few rights that he was effectively little more than a subject. So in France, after the French Revolution, where the ideal was that all men would also be citizens as part of their sacred status, different levels of citizenship, active and passive, were established. Even there man and citizen were distinct.

The distinction between human and citizen continues in the marked form of those effective slaves, the so-called guest workers, the illegal immigrants and, most poignantly, the children of illegal immigrants. This latter group exist fully nowhere and yet are found everywhere in the Western world. They are effective aliens in the country of their parents' origin, as they have no knowledge or sense of belonging there,[7] and are, as well, disenfranchised aliens in the country of their birth. The human rights they may enjoy are minimal, yet for all their humanity they are effectively and efficiently de-politicised. These are sharp cases but not unusual and not structurally dissimilar to all cases of de-politicisation.

In all these cases the source of the de-politicisation lies in drawing a distinction between human and citizen and understanding these terms in different ways. The distinction rests on requiring that the extension of these categories be distinct; that is to say what can be said of the citizen cannot automatically be said of the 'human'. That logical/political trick (for that is all it is) can be met fairly simply by declaring the term 'human' as non-political, the bearer of some minimal rights perhaps, and declaring the citizen as the political mode of being.

The consequence of such a device is to separate humanity from political being. This flies in the face of a wide range of thought from Dante, where *humanitas* was tied to *politizare,* through various models of civic republicanism and into Arendt, where to act politically is to achieve the highest state of the *vita activa.* This separation between humanity and political being has been developed into an art form in the modern and contemporary rupture between public and private. A classic form of de-politicisation is to maintain a distinction between *humanitas* and *politizare,* between human and citizen. A sharp distinction between the private and the public both produces and requires an ongoing de-politicisation.

Vice, 'Paradice' and Privacy

The idea of some kind of distinction between what one does in a public capacity and one's non-public affairs goes back to the *polis* and, in mythical form, to before that. In the *polis* it was the head of household, as a member of the *polis,* that partook in the common arena.[8] In practice sectional, tribal or other non-public interests frequently dominated public life. The measure of the fragility of the arrangement in which the public dominated can be determined from that brief moment in which the *polis* as an institution achieved its nobler aims. In its idealised form the *polis* was the domain of freedom, whereas the non-public domain, the household or the tribe was the domain in which traditional factors or necessity dominated. The non-public domains, no matter how important they might be in actual living, were not domains of freedom. By contrast freedom in the era of individualism, as that developed in Europe, came to be understood in predominantly private terms and in the development of civil society.

The inversion is significant in a variety of ways. It is also arguable that it is contained as a clear possibility within the founding moments. When, for example, St Paul appealed to the Emperor we see that duality which was expressed as the man of Tarsus and the citizen of Rome, but we hear little, if anything, of this citizenry which was based on the right of the protection of the Empire and to a trial by the Emperor. Taken in context this is hardly surprising for it is the protective role of being a citizen of Rome that mattered most in the narrative of his life and in the influence it had on subsequent affairs. And that protective element permitted the development of a private space. It was, after all, St Paul who developed the idea of that sense of individual mental and moral space that came to be known as *conscientia*, and it was *conscientia* in a more developed form that provided a foundation of the Protestant Reformation.

The development of individual moral space continued even through the revitalisation of civic values as they emerged in the formation of the guilds in twelfth- and thirteenth-century Germany. We hear much at this time of civic revitalisation and of pride in the city. Of the protective role of the city we also hear much. Of its actual effects on day-to-day living we hear little. This is not surprising for it was not the function of the city to provide in itself a domain of living – it was the function of the city to protect the emerging civil society within which meaningful life was effectively lived.

To say this is not to devalue the status of city membership. On the contrary its value was inestimable. The status of being a freeman was important to a certain kind of self-respect and a certain self-image. What was also important was that developing sense of personal identity, individuality and self-sufficiency that was provided primarily by those arrangements in civil society and that developed as a consequence of being a freeman. Guild membership, corporate membership, and the pride that came from that, are arrangements developed in civil society which depended on having the status of a member of the city and on the consequent protection of the city.

The consequence of the predominantly means–end value of the city is that we hear relatively little of the intrinsic value of civic virtue. This observation even applies to those paradigm cases of civic republicanism. Even within the context of the self-conscious civic republicanism of Bruni of the *Quattrocentro*, the value of extra-civic categories are frequently expressed. From Bruni we hear, in his melodious praises of the city and of the opportunities for the advancement of individuals regardless of social class, about the significance of particular classes, families and their role in furthering Florence as a great city. In a panegyric he praises Nanni Strozzi, a great general who died for the city, but he also makes it clear in his writings that it is a city supported by great families. In short, even in one of the noblest and finest expressions of the civic virtues, citizens are neither first or only citizens: they are *also* citizens.

That they can be regarded as also citizens is a conclusion that downgrades the moral significance of citizenship at the expense of increasing the private significance of morality. This was not difficult within the context of the grander expressions of civic republicanism, for even at its peak civic republicanism admits that there has been the development of a private moral space. Whereas in Greece the public–non-public distinction was between the public and the household, in the age of individualism it has come to be the public–private distinction. Against that backdrop Machiavelli's guillotine – the claim that public imperatives and private morality are distinct – is internally comprehensible.

A full public–private distinction, within which Machiavelli's claims, whether justifiable or not, make sense, as opposed to a more generic public–non-public distinction, requires the presence of a private space that is both individual and moral. It is individual in the modern sense and moral in the grasp that individuality obtains and maintains of a distinctive space of its own. A space for which it and it alone is ultimately responsible. Precursors to the public–private distinction are clearly there in the distinctions between *polis* and household, city and guild and similar couplets, but it is only as a consequence of the moral space arising with individualism as a distinct form that a clear re-drawing of the boundaries between the public and the non-public can be achieved in a way that makes sense in a contemporary context.

The primary force and point behind such a re-drawing is to bring about a relevant re-inversion and, in the process, to retain the importance of the private domain while reasserting the importance and significance of the public domain. The contemporary context recognises the value of the private domain, the private space and the development of individuality and self that arises from that space and which takes place in that space. Taken far enough such an outlook, if carried to extremes, may foster private morality and the development of private spaces at the expense of public concerns and public spaces. At its most extreme this outlook might come to place private space and private morality so much above other categories that there are no public imperatives.

If the public is entirely at the service of the private then it can become a slave to the private, the upshot of which is a peculiar kind of double inversion in which the public as an autonomous domain comes to disappear completely. In such a situation citizenship in any meaningful sense collapses into privacy.

There are a number of routes out of this dilemma. The first is to avoid the re-inversion by recapturing the public space, not by denying Machiavelli's guillotine or by denying the distinction between public and private, but by making it clear that while the function of the public is to protect the private it is also the function of the private to enhance the public. This requires fostering private and public or civic virtues and clarifying the effect that private actions have on public domains. Such an outlook is possible only if private and public can be clearly distinguished and if their causal links can be (no matter how fuzzily) specified. In short, what takes place in the private domain has public consequences and it matters and is significant that it has public consequences.

Second, the conception of what falls under the public domain might be widened so that more of what we do, regardless of the domain in which it formally falls, is treated as political. Additionally it would be possible to take the form of re-articulating what we do in our lives so that more of what we do, even if nominally private, is political in a wider sense.

Third, the distinction between public and private might be re-articulated. This would have the effect of moving citizenship from the formality of a domain separate from real living to the reality of actual living. If citizenship is a part of living, rather than a few actions performed in a domain, then citizenship becomes linked more directly to human relations and to the way or ways in which those relations are shared. Classically citizenship assumed that in the living of the family, the children, and the governance of slaves, the public domain did not, with some notable exceptions, interfere.[9] Conversely such living was not a part of citizenship.

In modern times that has led to the kind of view that the citizen is a juridically conceived public person but not a private person.[10] By contrast private actions are not the actions of citizens acting in a particular way, they are purely the actions of private persons. This distinction is at the very heart of liberal conceptions of politics and of citizenship.

There are a number of different conceptions of the relation between the public and private. Pushed to its extreme it has been argued that the citizen is formally distinct from the 'man'. Thus when the citizen and the man are distinguished, private and economic life is formally separated. This separation might work in a variety and multiplicity of ways but it is never complete, for even a private vice might have virtuous public consequences, as the classic lines from Mandeville make clear:

Thus every part was full of Vice,
Yet the whole mass a Paradice ...
And Vertue, who from Politicks
Had learn'd a Thousand cunning Tricks;
Was, by their happy Influence,
Made Friends with Vice: And ever since
The worst of all the Multitude
Did something for the common Good.[11]

There are multiple problems here, each of which is representative of contemporary difficulties.

First, one might take the view expressed by Erasmus that, 'For both the ruler and the subject private gain should not be a consideration.'[12] This assumes that private gain is a frequent cause of action but that in the role of ruler and subject it should be set aside in favour of the effect of the action in its conduciveness to the public good. The very idea that it is possible to set private gain aside in favour of the common good implies a conception of a split identity: an identity as a private person and an identity as a public person. It also implies sufficient unity of personality prior to the situation that a choice between the mode of being as private person and the mode of being as a public person could be made.

Second, even taking the formula in its own right there is a problem that requires explanation. If private vice could lead to public 'Paradice' then it might be thought that private vice should be considered an act of citizenship. Its effect on, and in, the public domain are significant, marked and, allegedly, positive. Yet acts of private vice were not then, and are not now, generally considered to be acts of citizenship. An act of private vice is primarily, even solely, a private act. It is not an act of public or civic virtue. An act of private vice might lead to a good but it is not a good in itself. It need not even be the case that the act should be intended to have good consequences. Such good consequences that do occur are a by-product of the act; they are part of its unintended consequences.

To split act and public consequence in this way depends on a model of act individuation that permits private consequences to be contained in the larger description of the act while excluding the larger public consequences from the act; they are a happy outcome but they are not part of any intended public virtue. Relatedly, public virtue, where that is understood as a deliberate and intended publicly good act, has little or no place in this model.

That these problems could occur is a direct consequence of splitting the private and public, as if they were distinct categories in the living of people, but it is also a consequence of splitting the intention and consequences of the act in a way that makes the practice of the civic virtues, at worst, impossible and, at best, difficult to describe.

The Mandeville model challenges the possibility of meaningful civic virtues. If those virtues are to be practised in a world where the public–private distinction is maintained in some way, some shift in the comprehension of action is required. First, it would be necessary to be able to describe and comprehend an ostensibly private act in terms of its public consequences, as Mandeville permits. Second, it would be necessary to be able to describe an act that was initially private in terms of both its private and publicly intended consequences. Third, it would be necessary to be able to describe an act that was intended to be publicly virtuous as virtuous or not regardless of whether the consequences were good or not. Fourth, it would be necessary to show how acts in either the private or public domain might be acts that were either particular, on the one hand, or, on the other hand, reached towards the universal. The latter point is crucial for even in a situation where the civic virtues are valued and well practiced there is no public monopoly on acting into the universal. On the contrary, civic virtue might be distorted and take its own values as universal, as the public yet particularistic idea of the *Volk*, for example, wrote itself as universal. By contrast an ostensibly private act might reach towards the universal, as in the claim found expressed in varying forms from Kant to Sartre that an action, any action, is an action for the world.

The first three of these concerns arises from restrictions in the notion of action. At its narrowest an act is any human event for which some intention can be located. The end point of that, however, is to be able to describe acts in increasingly narrow and increasingly detached terms. Thus 'I did not shoot the gun, I pulled the trigger' or 'I did not launch the missile, I turned the key' are claims that exhibit the moral distance, or, to use a slightly different terminology, the 'agentic shift' that becomes possible in a society that has and maintains distinct domains. Its end point is the Eichmann principle, iterated in the claim that 'I sat at my desk and did my business.' These three concerns are addressed in some way in the concept of the act-moment developed earlier. The notion of the act-moment relates the action to its hermeneutic and/or narrative background rather than permitting artificial and frequently merely convenient distinctions of what counts as an act to prevail. How that works in practice will depend on cases, but it would, for instance, require Eichmann to explain his actions in terms of the narrative that was the Nazi programme of world domination. Eichmann's claim is a case of removing an act from its wider consequence, of narrowing it to the point where no meaning and no responsibility attaches to it. The opposite is possible – namely, to place an act in its wider context so that what is normally described in narrow terms is re-described in wider terms and placed into a wider narrative. This is the first component in an action that is for the world. The second component is taking responsibility for that act. Taken together these components enable someone in the private domain to comprehend and, where appropriate, claim their act as an act that was not merely private but was also an act of civic virtue. The public domain does not have an exclusive monopoly on the public virtues.

This links to the fourth concern, that acts in either the public or the private domain might be either particular or universal in their orientation. Generally it is assumed that the public domain is the domain of the general or of the universal. It is the domain in which matters of common concern are expressed, and in which solutions to those concerns are developed. By contrast private acts are acts for oneself or for a sectional group of people; they are, therefore, particular. Obviously the automatic connection between public and universal and private and particular does not hold in the easy and ready sense attributed to it. If it did we would not have found the history of one people or peoples endlessly written on the world as world history. We would not have found that the destructive ideas of the *Volk* or similar notions were used to drive out alterity. Indeed if the public virtues are taken as acting into the universal then they are not automatically attached to any particular domain and are the exclusive privilege of no domain.

To disjoin the public and the universal and the private and the particular in this way is highly significant. Does an act reach towards that which is general, enduring and of little, if any, advantage to the actor or is it merely that which grasps immediate benefit and gratification? An otherwise private act might well be an act of citizenship, of deep citizenship, and an act in whatever domain that reaches towards an extended conception of humanity and humanism is not an act separate from the practice of the virtues. Relatedly, an otherwise private act which meets all those criteria is a choice for the world and is a virtuous act.

Of course no one can leave their particularity behind – it is the very condition of their living and the condition in which they find themselves when seeking the universal. By contrast to live entirely in the particular is to be so engaged in the immediacies of the world that it is to have no life at all. The basic condition of lying between the particular and the universal is part of the human condition and is a condition of politics itself. The political is not confined to the public domain as that is classically understood. To act from one's particular condition of living to a condition beyond those confines is to act politically and virtuously – it is the ethico-political moment. It is in the creation and re-creation of the ethico-political moment that the civic virtues can be most readily practised and in its creation and re-creation that the moral space required as a condition of selfhood can emerge. Taken together, the moral space of selfhood and the public space within which action is instanced provide the structure and foundation for the citizen self.

The implication of this is that politics, citizenship and the virtues might occur in a wide variety of places and occur as a development in the manifold aspects of living a particular life. To live a particular life is necessary, but it does not follow from that necessity that one need be always and only dominated by the most immediate and most selfish components of that life. A life must be led in a particular way but it does not follow from that necessity that it cannot reach towards the common, the general or the universal across a range of activities. That reach towards the general or the universal is not necessarily completed, or even significantly assisted, merely by having the formality of a public domain; on the contrary it is often and sometimes most tellingly and fetchingly found in actions that seem not to be in that domain at all. To move towards governing one's life with respect to general concerns is reasonable and possible. To live a particular life and reach in it towards the universal is a reasonable goal of life. If that is done in a worldly rather than an unworldly way it is an act of the citizen self.

A Being in Moral Space

There is an ambiguity in the concept of the citizen self, for one pole of the term pulls outwards towards the world while the other turns the opposite way into the inner recesses of the mind – St Augustine's 'inner citadel'. In standard conceptions of these terms nothing is more private than the self and nothing more public than the citizen. Yet it is with just this condition of tension that Western political life, after St Augustine's discovery of the radically reflexive self, has had to cope.

Self-awareness always occupies a position of in-betweenness or *metaxy*. It has been expressed and re-expressed utilising a variety of metaphors and in a variety of ways. It is to straddle the cities of the just and the unjust, as Herodotus conceived it; to live in two cities, the city of light and the city of darkness, as Augustine of Hippo expressed it; to live between reason and faith, as with Aquinas; to be caught up in an eternal and cosmic war between the forces of light and the forces of darkness, as the Zoroastrians, the Manicheans and the directors of *Star Wars* had it; or more commonly and more mundanely, but no less significantly, to be caught up in day-to-day living, while being conscious of that and of one's own finitude. It is the space and place of tension between the particular and the universal.

The space and place between the particular and the universal is not a single point on a single spectrum. There are numerous such points and numerous such spectrums. The variety of expressions for the *metaxial* condition exhibits the variety of the condition. Relatedly there is no reason why everyone should be at the same point on any particular *metaxial* spectrum. For instance, someone engaged completely in day-to-day living will be concerned primarily with particularities, while someone engaged in living as a contemplative or living life directed towards the unworldly will be concerned primarily with universalities. Each is a mode of living, even possibly, in certain circumstances, a witness to a certain sort of Being.

At one extreme there is the life of the religious: the seeker after nirvana. This path, and respect for it, is found in almost all major societies, and all major world religions make allowance for and even encourage it. Such an existence is an exercise in, and a witness to, living close to the sentiment of the universal. But however close the contemplative might come to the universal it will never be achieved. By contrast someone might attempt to abandon all universal principles and live on an almost day-to-day basis, drawing their principles and aims, if any, from a restricted range of objectives. Arthur Miller's *Death of a Salesman*[13] illustrates this well, and Oliver Sacks describes how the idiot savant seems scarcely able to generalise.[14] The genius of the idiot savant, it seems, is often the genius of an excess of particularity, a rare talent that does not relate to other aspects of living.

In all these cases we admire those who reach towards the universal end of the *metaxial* spectrum and are suspicious or disdainful of those who reach towards the particular end of that spectrum. The reason for this is complex, but among other factors it is clear that to live entirely at the particular end of the *metaxial* spectrum is to live without principle or without significant or appropriate principle. The self-contained principles of a salesman, for instance, are not, by themselves, cause for wider admiration, and the talents of the idiot savant might produce wonder but no real envy. Relatedly, and to return to an earlier point, to perceive government as merely the management of affairs is not one of the finer indications of *noblesse humanitas*.

Living with principle involves living with some conception of acting into the universal, while knowing that the universal will never be achieved. It implies living with and not resolving the *metaxial* condition. This uneasy condition is the foundation of politics and the foundation of radical democracy. The in-between condition is always an incomplete condition, and it is upon incompleteness that politics thrives and upon its incompleteness that a movement towards its recovery can be commenced if not completed. For that reason social arrangements that seek their own completion, as some absolutist, and all totalitarian – conditions seek completion and closure, are inimical to politics, to citizenship and to self. By contrast social arrangements that are open provide the conditions in which politics, citizenship and self may be fostered.

It is in socially and politically incomplete situations, in fractured not in unitary societies, that a strong sense of self is developed. It is in the circumstances of fractured societies that the self is required to find some principle of unification or fall towards fragmentation. Consciousness might, among other conditions, be expressed in ideal typical terms as unitary, fractured or unified: none of which are likely to be found in perfect form in experience. A unitary consciousness is primarily unreflective and is a condition out of which a clear sense of self is unlikely to develop. A fractured consciousness is, by contrast, a consciousness that is open to the vagaries of experience without any means of organising that experience. A unified consciousness is a condition within which the varieties of experience are subsumed into a set of principles that relate them no matter how uneasily. It is the latter condition, the condition of a unified consciousness, that is the condition most likely to produce a strong sense of self. It is fractured times that generate the possibility for complex and unified but not unitary selves to arise in, on, and out of the fractures. The ambiguities of fractured times permit conditions within which further and often unconventional public spaces emerge. The discovery of principles of unification, of acting on principle, is what defines the self. It is for this reason that the self as an object in moral space requires both unificatory principles and the opportunity and actuality of acting on principle. It can do neither of these without acting outwards, away from particular interests that it may have and towards wider world concerns, towards the universal. To be is not only to be political it is to be a citizen in the sense of acting outwards and away from the condition of immediacy.

This pushes the concept of citizenship in three directions. First, to the idea of the human-citizen; second, to that of balancing the demands of immediacy against the requirements of principled abstractions; and, third, to that of the condition of *metaxy* represented in the spectrum of being that lies between the particular and the universal.

In the first case, if the distinction between the categories of human and citizen is too severe or too great then either one or both of the categories of 'human' and 'citizen' would disappear altogether, or they would emerge in an unacceptable tension. If they were extensionally distinct to the extent that it was possible to be a human or to be a citizen without these categories sharing any significant predicates, then the categories of human and citizen would be torn apart and ruptured. In that case the *metaxial* condition would

break down. In practice this frequently occurs. The case of stateless
or citizenless people is well known to wrench citizen and human
apart.[15] Such 'strangers among us' have human rights but no
meaningful share in public activity.

In the second case there is, to use the jargon of the present, a
fault line that has developed between the reality of distinctions based
on divisions such as social class, race, gender, ethnic group and
the formality of citizenship. When citizenship in its classic form is
taken as the prime category it is not citizenship that appears as an
artificial category it is rather that class, race, gender, ethnic group
and other social situations appear as arbitrary, artificial and *non-
relevant* distinctions. But in so appearing they inhibit the development
of deep citizenship – of a mode of citizenship that reaches beyond
such immediacies and to more general concerns.

In the third case, when particular actions appear as merely
particular actions governed by selfishness, sectionality or sectarian
concerns, they become devoid of larger meaning. The end point of
that is a diminished society where the diminished life of the strangely
principled but dead salesman and the meaningless talent of the idiot
savant without the redeeming, if limited, features of that talent
become characteristic of that diminished society. In either case these
characteristics fail to translate the experience of one domain, or one
mode of thought to another domain or another mode of thought;
the consequence of which is an inability to critically examine actions
in one domain from the perspective of another domain.

The counter to that limitation is not to enhance the living in one
domain by relying on it alone but to seek to live in a number of
different domains as, for instance, an individual; a member of an
ethnic group; a gendered person; a citizen of country 'x'; a citizen
of country 'y'; a citizen of the world; a human; a participant in world
creation; a member of the cosmos; and an individual whose actions
impact on the world, and so on.

This implies existing in a number of different domains and
existing in those domains in a unique and unparalleled way. It also
implies that the identity that one forges should not be taken entirely
from a single source. At best that produces a unitary identity; at
worst it produces no significant identity at all. The ambiguity of
formal political loyalties enhance more than debilitate this process.
To be a multiple citizen may be to live in multiple conditions of
ambiguity but that condition is more freedom enhancing than
restricting.

From the perspective of any particular state it may appear as undesirable to have multiple political loyalties, for it reduces the undivided
loyalty which that state might otherwise expect. From the point of
view of the individual the possession of multiple political loyalties
enhances ambiguity and the possibility of an escape from the

prisons of selfish, sectional and sectarian interests. Selfish, sectional and sectarian interests are the deepest challenge to deep citizenship. If actions are taken and justified only on such grounds then neither self nor citizenship will develop in any meaningful way.

The development of self and citizenship requires both a conception of a moral space within which action is possible and a clear sense that action which arises from immediate concerns, but that also reaches beyond those concerns, is possible. To act into the universal is not only required for citizenship – it is required for the generation of that moral space in which a sense of self that can be said to be one's own may emerge. The opposite of that enlarged position as a position of moral and political contraction is always possible but it will always be a position without principle, a position without moral space, and in consequence a lack of developed self and with it the clear possibility of an absence of deep citizenship. Self and virtue are always in a set of necessary and inseparable tensions and virtue is always practised against a set of civic contexts.

The plural nature of those contexts is important for it is in contexts not merely in a context that the modern civic virtues are practised and the self becomes distinguished as a unified but multi-faceted being in moral space. Multiple contexts create multiple tensions for the self, but they are also the source of its development. To be a citizen of a number of multiple realms is to add to ambiguity and in-betweenness, but this is not to reduce freedom – it is to add to it. To be engaged in such a multi-threaded existence is similarly to add to the possibilities of freedom. None of these possibilities are without their dangers for they may result in such a concern with the immediate that the development of person and personality is thwarted. But such restriction is not necessary. The opposite possibility is also present and enlargement of action and self might relatedly emerge. In turning away from the mere particular and in acting into the universal, however that may be expressed, there is the opportunity for self and politics to come together in a meaningful and valuable way.

In general terms what this implies, among other things, is the construction and acceptance of a set of structures and a set of cultural expectations that provide a high degree of congruence between the categories of 'human' and 'citizen'. To live one's life, to relish its particularity while also reaching towards the universal, is not to weaken one's grip on the particular: it is to enhance it, to place it in a wider context, to see its relation to other wider contexts and to see how it intersects with the lives of others. To live in a condition of *metaxy*, to embrace and accept it, to attempt to resolve this uneasiness by not resolving it at all, but by living with it on an ongoing basis, is the challenge for contemporary politics and for the thoughtful, political self.

6

The New *Polis*

The ideal of living the political or the civic life as part of being human has traditionally been based on the idea of the city. It is the city that furnishes the public space without which shared experience and common ground cannot be found. In consequence the city has represented the general or universal in the lives of its citizens. I have suggested that frequently this general or universal has been little more than another set of disguised particularisms. This is notably the case in those arrangements which have written world history in their own image or have taken the history or experience of one group of people as representative of other peoples. The opposite error, however, is found in the claim that all living is mere particularity. To live such a life would be a life devoid of principle, virtue and self. Self and virtue are interrelated, so the practice of the political life, the civic virtues and the idea and practice of acting for common goods, imperfectly formed though that concept may be, are ideas and practices that enlarge the mind. 'To think from the perspective of everyone else' might be one of those Kantian maxims that seem impossible, but to think from other perspectives is necessary for the enlargement of the mind and the enlargement of the critical faculties. One consequence of that enlargement has been the critique of Western history as world history. That history contained within it the very maxims that undercut its world historical ideas and practices. The phoenix that emerges from those ashes is a multitude of histories and diverse voices. The political life is not to be obtained merely by being one of those particular voices but by being a voice behind which there is an enlarged outlook, and the place of the city in this development is clear enough.

Living in the city and learning to orient oneself to more than immediate sectional concerns is a valuable foundation for an enlarged mind. The point is repeated time and again throughout the theory of the city. Setting aside 'my' concerns in favour of 'our' concerns is central to the gods of Mesopotamia, as they met in assembly; to the *polis* of Athens, as evidenced in Solon, Plato, Aristotle, Zeno; to the rhetoric of the Roman Republic; to the City of God; into Dante's *humanitas;* Rousseau's 'Social Contract'; and any and all injunctions to set sectional interest aside. It is this

8

shared life of the city which permitted some development of the idea of the common and with the practice of attending to it.

Conversely when the city collapsed, so citizenship in the sense of the practice and participation in common life collapsed. As a clear common life collapsed and individualism emerged so the value of the civic virtues diminished. In opposition to the value of the civic virtues the development of individualism placed polity at the service of individuality. So for Hobbes, one of the founders of liberal modes of thought, the primary purpose of the state became, first, to serve that most ultimate of private interests, the protection of life, and, second, to protect private and sectional interests. That basic idea expressed by Hobbes became, in a variety of forms, a central tenet of liberalism. The end point of the decline of the public virtues is to be found in the Mandeville principle: the view that private vice leads to public good.

It may be that the decline of the *polis* has led to an inevitable and irreversible decline in the civic virtues and with it citizenship. Certainly, if Wolin's claim that 'with the decline of the polis, politics lost its context'[1] is correct, then the prospects for citizenship would be dismal indeed. Such a claim and such a concern rests on, among other things, the decline of assembly consequent on the growth of mass society. Clearly the members of mass society cannot know each other on a face to face basis, as Aristotle seems to think desirable, and clearly not all issues can be debated by every member of society.

The changes from the *poleis*, the classic republics and the governments of cities to the growth and development of large-scale societies may appear to end the context of politics and with it both politics and meaningful citizenship. The rise of representative democracies seems adequate empirical evidence that politics has been removed from the life of people and with it the decline of the civic virtues associated with significant concepts of citizenship. Representation removes direct political action from the individual and shifts it to some other. The end point of that model is the loss of politics, the decline of the domain within which the virtues could be practised, the actual decline of those virtues and the end of citizenship.

This would be the outcome if citizenship and politics ended up in a merely representative mode. I have, however, suggested that politics can be practised across a number of domains and that even sectional and particular interests can be seen in a general and universalistic perspective. This offers two divergent possibilities. One is an irreversible decline of meaningful citizenship, the other is a recapturing of that concept and with it the possibility of renewing the civic virtues. The argument here is for the latter.

Regaining the Public Domain

Liberal democracy and the practice of the civic virtues in a deep and active sense are generally taken as broadly incompatible.[2] The reasons for this are clear enough. A prime function of liberal democratic individualism is to protect individuals and that kind of individual association characteristic of civil society. Relatedly, a prime function of the liberal state is to contain and define what counts as politics removing it as much as possible from individuals and individual associations. By contrast the function of civic republicanism is to engage the population as much as possible in common and public affairs. The incompatibility is not just logical and structural, it is also historically foundational. It is found in embryonic form in the social originary, where the gods spoke for themselves on the one hand but represented others, cities, for example, on the other. The split between direct and representative politics is an incompatibility backed up by two and a half millennia of understandings. I will argue that the split need not continue if a prime function of constitutional liberal democracies is taken to be creating and maintaining the framework for private action, civil associations and civil society, as in the classic understanding, and also permitting the creation and maintenance of new political spaces of political society.

On the model I propose a re-contextualised function of liberalism is to promote *politizare*, *qua* Dante. Such an argument is perfectionist but only to the extent of understanding that the political participation in one's own life and in its conditions is a significant part of *humanitas*. It does not prescribe any particular conduct or propose any particular programme: it leaves that as the outcome of the deliberation occurring in the new *agon*.

Such a model of a reclaimed citizenship needs to take into account the problems, promises and potentials of citizenship as found in the classic civic model from the pantheon onwards and in the more detached and status-oriented model of citizenship found in mass society. The problems, promises and potentials are almost endless. I take a few as central. This is not to deny the existence of others or to claim that the list is exhaustive, but to suggest that there are a number of central characteristics that have provided serious difficulties for the concept of citizenship in one or other or both of the classic or modern models that can be isolated. I shall show first that each of these characteristics has generally led to difficulties for citizenship and for civically responsible outlooks. But I shall also show that these difficulties are contingent and not necessary; the implication of that being that they can be transcended. However, I go further than that, and show that what appear as difficulties can actually be utilised as the foundation of a new citizenship. What appears initially as a set of major weaknesses turns out to be a set of major strengths, and that together with other features present in late modernity they can now form the basis of a revitalised political life.

Characteristic of the change from traditional conceptions of civic life to mass society has been: first, the growth of individual consciousness and the sense of self that might go along with that; second, and relatedly, the fragmentation of society; third, the growth of the modern state; fourth, in some jurisdictions at least, the growth of liberal democratic structures; and fifth, the ambiguities in life that emerge as a consequence of rifts and fractures in the previous four components.

These factors, and their ambiguities, permit the development of forms of space both actual and virtual that are neither entirely private nor entirely public. This process can be enhanced by recasting the social imaginary to bring that which is not currently regarded as political into the domain of the political. No doubt the characteristics listed above could be extended, but I take these as fundamental to the decline of any reasonable conception of citizenship. Each would have to be dealt with in some way if politics was to be recaptured. A failure to deal with these factors would almost certainly mean that the recovery of politics would either be impossible or would need to be revolutionary and not merely, as I am suggesting, radical. Each of the aspects on the list are normally taken as inhibiting the growth and development of politics or as leading to a loss of the possibility of ever reclaiming the civic virtues. The claim here is to the opposite effect: each contains within it the possibility of reclaiming politics and citizenship, albeit in new and radical ways.

The relation between consciousness and civility in that larger sense so beloved by Hobbes and made by him the basis of society[3] is clear. Without some shared manners, some shared conception of how to behave towards one another, communication is impossible. Such common manners come readily in the city in which members are internally related to each other. They come with much greater difficulty in society where individuals stand externally related to each other and when it is external structures that maintain them. In situations of mass society consciousness is different from the consciousness of the classic city. The change from the classic city to mass society was accompanied by a change in the nature of consciousness – in particular the growth of individual conceptions of the self.

The changing nature of consciousness, in particular the development of individualism, is usually taken to be incompatible with, or at least to rest uneasily with, the growth of the civic virtues. The reasons are clear enough. Classic models of citizenship did not invoke or depend on an individual conception of self, or virtue. On the contrary they rested on shared conceptions of the psyche. Classic

Greek formulations of mind show mind and consciousness as dispersed.[4] This did not eliminate notions of responsibility but it did not take responsibility and cognate notions in a merely or crudely individualistic sense. The city was not a collection or set of autonomous individuals prior to the city but people who comprehended themselves in relation to their place in the city. They were not individuals externally related to the city but people internally related to each other and the city. By contrast individualism in the sense of a radically reflexive self, to use Taylor's phrase,[5] was a product of the massive social breakdown at the end of the Roman Empire. The effects of this breakdown, combined with the genius of St Augustine, led to an articulation of the individual as an object in moral space. The idea is expressed most fully in the doctrine of individual justification: that it was the individual who was personally accountable to God for their actions.

The structural conditions that led to a decline of the ideal of the unitary city and to the growth of mass society are also the conditions that led to an increase in the conception of the individual self. All the elements of the idea of individual subjectivity and individual moral accountability are trailed in St Augustine's writings, but it was the fragmentation of society following the feudal breakdown that produced the fully-fledged radically-reflexive self as the foundation of the new social order.

Individuals are not the stuff of which classic cities are made and the decline of the civic virtues is not due merely to the decline of the cities. It is also due to the emergence of individuals. Individuals are the products of fracture, of a detachment from their social basis, and do not constitutively contain the elements required to undo their lot. The modern state is an appropriate device with which to contain the individual elements of a fragmented society. It is not for nothing that Hobbes is the theorist *par excellence* of political modernity. A modern society is fragmented and fractured. This is not merely an accidental component of such societies it is basic to them. The individualism produces cross-cutting loyalties, arrangements and associations. Differences of status, occupation, class and sectional interests produce varieties of homogeneity in certain respects and heterogeneity in other respects. The sum of this is fracture and fissure rather than holism and unity.

Once again it is the modern state that keeps or attempts to keep the fragments together in some way. A clear demand made by the state in the pursuit of that task is of overriding loyalty. Sectional and other interests may contain some loyalties and some claims. Civil arrangements and association of contract contain legitimate claims backed by state, family, friendship and ties of blood. But the abiding and overriding loyalty is that claimed by the state. There is nothing especially modern in this general principle, as we see clearly in Antigone, in Socrates, in Jesus and in other examples. But the sheer force of the claims of the modern secular state, distinguished from any claims it makes on behalf of either God, the gods, or community, is breathtaking. It is breathtaking in its power, force and extent. It overrides almost all other claims, permitting at most and exceptionally, and with great reluctance, the effects of conscience to limit some of its claims.

The modern state has incorporated some of the characteristics of citizenship into its structure in the development of representative democracy. Representative democracy provides the members, that is the individuals of the nation state, a status. It permits them some formal activity, primarily the right to stand as a representative and the right to vote for a representative, some protection and, within carefully prescribed limits, freedom of association.

The fifth characteristic of the shift from traditional conceptions of civic life to mass society lies in the ambiguities that arise as a consequence of the rifts and fractures generated by and in modern society and by and in the modern state. Max Weber, that darkest of prophets of the modern bureaucratic rational state, had a nightmare in which the rational state brought everything under its control. The nightmare is understandable. It also founders on the failure of rationality to deal with the issue of judgment. Judgment, according to Kant, is of two types, determinate and reflective.[6] In the former, known cases are brought under pre-existing rules. In the latter, unknown cases have to be dealt with without reference to any pre-existing rules. In a dynamic society the need for reflective judgment will occur on a continuing basis. But the exercise of such judgment, which, according to Arendt,[7] is the most political of our mental faculties, brings judgment and action together in an ethico-political act-moment.

This requirement for the ongoing use of reflective judgment occurs as a consequence of the inability of the modern state ever to be able to entirely specify the precise nature of actions required in that part of society over which it claims control. That failure is a necessary and not a contingent feature of the modern state. It is not a mere failure of mechanism but is built into the nature of an individualised yet collective and dynamic human action. What this implies, among other things, is that the state, no matter how much it attempts to control and regulate the activities of its own bureaucracy and no matter how hard it attempts to control and regulate activities in civil society, will always underspecify the nature and content of actions. A further consequence is that modern individuals will always be faced with decisions to make for which there are no rules and guidelines and will always be faced with the ethico-political act-moment.

Clearly the possibilities for the ethico-political act-moment to occur and re-occur can be enhanced or inhibited. It is perfectly possible to imagine a state, both in the sense of institution and condition, in which the conditions of reflective judgment were fostered rather than inhibited. To foster judgment requires the state to limit its activities but where it does regulate such regulation should be concerned with, among other things, protecting those spaces within which reflective judgment takes place.

The individualism characteristic of modern society might undercut citizenship but it also provides the possibility of an expanded consciousness which permits the emergence of places and spaces within which the civic virtues can be developed. The hallmark of that expanded consciousness is found in the ability to take one's own private and/or sectional interests and measure them against other perspectives – Kant's maxim to see things from the perspective of others or the notion of acting into the universal. That possibility emerges from individualism and is the foundation of an individualism that permits, even develops, the conditions for and the possibility of a renewed understanding of the civic virtues.

There are a number of elements in the shift from city to society that have been taken as inimical to citizenship. Among these are the growth of individual consciousness, and the sense of self that might go along with that; the fragmentation of society; the growth of the modern state; the growth of liberal democratic structures; and the ambiguities in life arising from a variety of rifts and fractures. Yet it turns out that these elements, rather than being necessarily inimical to citizenship, provide the foundation for a model of citizenship that includes all the classic civic virtues while being more inclusive than the original models. The foundation of such an enhanced citizenship is a genuine model of individualism, with all the individual responsibility that goes with that: the requirement of such individuals is that they make reflective judgments. Such reflective judgments are what I call ethico-political act-moments. There is nothing inconsistent with this and the emergence of the nation state. On the contrary the nation state, generally regarded as preserving and protecting civil society and civil association, can be perfectly well regarded as preserving and protecting new forms of extra-statist political association. That over-arching protective role is possible as part of the generation of the new *poleis*. A clear practical implication of that is for the state not to condemn so-called extra-parliamentary activity but to welcome, foster and protect it.

The elements of modern society that are taken as counting against the development of the civic virtues can be turned around to become components within which the civic virtues can be developed, albeit in a distinctively contemporary sense. There is no need, as MacIntyre suggests,[8] to seek a new St Benedict for the elements of the new civic virtues 'are already among us'. A fragmented society might offer fracture alone but it might, by contrast, offer a variety of places, spaces and ambiguities within which politics, citizenship and freedom can be exercised. Social and cultural rifts, fractures and pluralities of views and purposes produce a plurality of spaces and places, locking, intersecting and overlapping to the extent that it becomes difficult to speak of a single public space. By contrast it becomes easier to speak of a multitude of public spaces and a multitude of publics and of a number of *poleis*.

Those places, spaces and publics need not rely on traditional conceptions of spatiality and phenomenological immediacy. There are a variety of ways in which people communicate with each other and across a range of time-scales that make the idea of the immediacy of presentation and the immediacy of the present somewhat notional. A notional, or even in some cases virtual, present might be nonetheless effective as a basis for communication and for agonistic, if spatially and temporally distant, relations. It is too early to say what the full effect of virtuality and cyber-space might be in terms of the exchange of views required for democratic intersection and interaction, but it is also too early to preclude such relations as neither agonistic or democratic on the grounds that they do not fit the standard temporal and spatial models.

Reclaiming citizenship is possible, for the fragmentation of society has produced places and spaces which permit both the obtaining of a variety of different and distinct vantage points as well as that growth of individual consciousness which can potentially come together as the citizen self. Such a mode of being is possible when someone who in acting for and taking responsibility for its self acts into the universal in a manner sufficient to set sectionalism, sectarianism and selfishness aside. Such action is possible due to the opportunity for and the capacity for a variety of outlooks and perspectives resulting from the fragmentation of society. Each of those outlooks and perspectives is part of the development of alternative perspectives: perspectives that while critical of others are also critical of self. And that which is critical of self is enlarging of self. The upshot is the enlargement of mind that Kant sought. It is also the individualistic foundation of deep citizenship.

It turns out that individualism *per se* is not necessarily inimical to citizenship but may on the contrary lead to a growth of self and a growth of different perspectives that are supportive of the civic virtues. These perspectives and aspects taken with the fragmentation of society generate the possibility of new political spaces and the development of political as well as civil society. This is a foundation of multiple political spaces, new *poleis* and regions of deep citizenship in new spaces and places.

The new *poleis* depends in part on those new individuals of the late twentieth century: decentred individuals. There are a variety of ways in which individuality can develop. I shall deal with centred and decentred individualism. Centred individualism is best characterised in the Cartesian value which takes the individual as prior to society. At its extreme, centred individualism places individuals at the centre of the universe. The individual is centre stage. Its philosophical foundation is in the *cogito* of Descartes;[9] its political foundation is in the a-social being of Hobbes's natural condition of mankind. When Descartes took a sceptical line and argued that he was a thinking substance he placed himself at the centre of the universe. Cartesian individuals are centred individuals for they take it that their existence is a central part of the universe, which they precede in some significant way(s). They take it that the world in which they find themselves is the creation of individual action and ingenuity. Hobbes continues the same general kind of argument, so from experience and argument it is possible to show the priority of the individual and the secondary nature of society. In general terms, albeit with significant internal variations, the same kind of argument can be found in Kant and from all these sources into classic liberal thought.

By contrast decentred individualism starts from the premise of human sociality. There is a line of argument from Hegel and Marx, and from Wittgenstein and Schutz, into communitarianism and some post-modern arguments, in which individual consciousness is shown to be a social product. This view of individuality varies markedly in the residue that is left to the individual. In all cases it is seen that consciousness is obtained or largely obtained and developed in actual social situations.

This thesis can be developed in two quite distinct ways. It might be taken as what I shall call the strong sociality thesis which sees the individual as so much a product of social factors that the decentred individual is effectively no individual at all. The assumption is that that which is a product of society is reducible to the social forces and processes of which they are a part. This would be the case if the intersubjective process that went into individual consciousness fully determined that consciousness.

The thesis might, alternatively, be taken in a weaker sense as indicating that the process of intersubjectivity, while significant in the development of consciousness is, however, underdeterminative of the final consciousness. There are a variety of reasons that could be offered in support of the weaker thesis, some of which I have already mentioned. Principal among these reasons is that in open and fractured societies unique characteristics of individuality come to overlay that intersubjectivity. On this model the decentred individual can be part of and partly formed by society, yet be free in the sense of having his or her actions and consciousness underdetermined by society. Such an individual can, by acting in a variety of domains, come to have a wide variety of perspectives, none of which is completely dominates.

Generally, modest social fractures, faults, rifts and ruptures provide the opportunity for consciousness to develop in one of two ways. In the first way it sinks into its own particularity, placing its own experience as the only legitimate experience, while in the second, it utilises the opportunities of varied outlooks provided by the rifts to develop alternative viewpoints. The former leads to selfishness, sectionalism and sectarianism, the latter leads to the possibility of autonomous action and empowerment. That autonomous action and empowerment develops in conjunction with the growth of a certain sort of individuality on the one hand and the opportunity to exercise it on the other. The enhancement of empowered individuality includes, among other features, the power to act, the power to provide appropriate and meaningful interpretations of what one is doing: to be, as I put it earlier, a poet in one's own life and to meaningfully affirm and take responsibility for self and actions. All of these capacities rest on having the ability to critically judge oneself from alternative perspectives, to critically take the perspectives of others and engage in the enlargement of the mind. These features are required in order to be able to act towards the universal without which there can be no reaching beyond selfishness, sectionalism and sectarianism, no cultivation of the civic virtues, and no deep citizenship.

The politically conscious but social self and deep citizen turns out to be interrelated as a citizen self, for being a deep citizen is acting in one or many of the various spaces of appearances in which one finds oneself. It spurns confinement to a role or domain provided by the state. The multitude of spaces provides a real opportunity to participate in the operation of one's own life and to exhibit both *politizare* and *humanitas* in a variety of places and a multitude of spaces. Such possibilities depend on a reconstructed individualism but they also require reconstructed political possibilities within which political activity, as *politizare*, can be exercised.

Political Society

The space for *politizare* is to be found either within the confines of the state or without it. If the former, it is statist and concerned with statecraft or some aspect of it, in which case it is either not political or political only in a limited sense; if the latter, it is social and similarly not political. I have already argued that politics construed in statist terms has limited both the conception and practice of politics.

Here, I want to examine an argument that politics has more or less disappeared as a consequence of the rise of the social and argue that, on the contrary, the rise of the social has generated new political possibilities. They are, however, possibilities that are fully realised only when individual interest is widened beyond the immediate concerns of the individual. Another way of putting this is that individual interests can be part of the practice of the civic virtues within the context of deep citizenship: of reaching towards the universal while not losing sight of the actualities of living.

Hannah Arendt, in one of the most influential analyses of our contemporary political predicament, centres political action on what she calls the 'space of appearances'.[10] The space of appearances is that area between people in which they exercise and exhibit their individuality and their mutuality. The two aspects are necessary to each other. Without a plural individuality there can be no mutuality and without mutuality the individuals would not be individuals in the plural. If they existed at all it would be in different effective universes: they would be able to say and have nothing to say to each other.

On Arendt's account political action is distinctively human. Such a view is part of a long tradition. The tradition as descended from Athens, symbolically speaking, is to take politics as central to life. The tradition as descended from Jerusalem, symbolically speaking, is to take spirituality as central to life. There is an odd moment when they come together in that celebration of the Fall given by Dante when Adam's disobedience, his willing, acting and being in command of his own life, was treated not as a sin to be regretted but as a defining moment of humanity.

Such claims are neither purely empirical nor purely normative – they are descended from some part of the social originary and are part of the story that people in communities tell to each other and which they transmit in tradition in order to make the world and make sense of their place in it. In this case the story as descended from some part of the social originary has become in a variety of ways part of the preconception of what it is to be fulfilled as a human. To be human in this sense is not a biological term or a species term, or at least not a biological or species term alone. To be human in the senses used in these cases is to have certain non-biological attributes and to be able to express them. That expression requires a forum and that forum, when it is worldly, can take place only among others. It is being in the world with others that provides the forum – the space of appearances, to utilise Arendt's term.

On Arendt's analysis the space of appearances is met not in society, but in a distinct political arena. Society or *oikos*, in the Greek model (from which the notion of economy is derived), was concerned with household affairs and partial rather than common or universal interests. By contrast the political arena provided the conditions within which action was possible and revelation to self and others could occur. This agonistic model of politics is, perhaps, one of the purest types of political action conceivable. The difficulty is that where that distinct agonistic arena is lacking then it would seem that politics is lacking. If that kind of reasoning were carried through then citizenship and the opportunities for politics and citizenship of a meaningful kind would now be absent. This does seem to be a central thrust of Arendt's claim, and the contemporary world as she sees it is now concerned largely with matters of economy or housekeeping. The agonistic arena and with it political possibilities have disappeared.

Arendt draws attention to the diminution of politics in the conditions of modernity for, on her analysis, society is at best nonpolitical and at worst even anti-political. The conclusion, that politics has been eliminated by, or at least diminished by, the rise of society, is significant but it does not follow that there can be no transformation that permits politics in society. It is more the converse. Society has become politicised. The space of appearances may well have disappeared but the appearance of spaces has multiplied. The variety and number of spaces of appearance in a fragmented society is bewildering. It ranges from the coffee-house culture of early bourgeois society, the development of the printing press that permitted extended dialogue, the growth of newspapers, books, current affairs magazines, liberal education, radio and television news and current affairs programmes, to the growth of computerised interchanges and exchanges, and the development of virtual space(s), virtual cities, virtual conversations, extended dialogues, chattering classes, single-issue pressure groups, consumer revolts, ethical share buying, talk radio, protests, demonstrations, and countless other forms of expression.

In all of these situations and in all of these cases people interact and exchange views. Frequently they do not do so on a face to face basis. Frequently they do not even do so in a way that reflects even some immediacy of simultaneity. A conversation on a topic might be extended over quite lengthy periods of time as an exchange of letters in a newspaper or an exchange of views on a computer bulletin board, but it is an exchange for all that. It may be extended across the globe and across weeks or even months of time, but again it is an exchange for all that.

The bewildering spaces of appearance are simultaneously places for exchanges of experiences: they are spaces of experience. And it is in such spaces that the mind is enlarged. It is also a space, even if virtual, in which all of plurality, individuality, mutuality and the other components of action that Arendt finds as central to politics can and often do occur. They are social but they are far from merely social for they raise and encompass all the characteristics of political action in the agonistic sense and they are far from merely statist: it is rather a hallmark of the new politics.

The new politics, the development of deep citizenship and the citizen self, occurs not in spite of but because of the social: it occurs as a consequence of shifting the political into the social. This is the moment of politicising the social, of newly creating a political society, or re-enforcing the trends towards a political society that are already present in European society, the history of which has been racked with tension in which a tradition of debate, discussion, dissension, conformity and non-comformity has developed. There is no significant point in the history of the West, even at its most monolithic, when there was not some challenge to the prevailing orthodoxy of the day. Nor was there ever a time when the prevailing orthodoxy did not have to be fought over before it became such. A consequence of such contests is a politics emerging from individual debate and from the fractures between social tendencies, social groups and social forces. It is in just those fractures and rifts that individuals having distinct views emerge and the ground for non-statist politics is laid. There is a non-trivial sense in which it can be argued that politics is a Western invention. There is a non-trivial sense in which it can be said that politics is built into the tensions of the West. And there is a non-trivial sense in which politics in the West can be said to be in a condition of resurgence – when its new spaces have become the new contexts for politics, the new *poleis*.

Statecraft and Politics

The argument so far has assumed that politics, Dante's *politizare*, is a good in itself. To act politically, to take charge of significant and meaningful aspects of one's life in the company of others and to have some share in the conditions of that life, is good not merely as a means to some further end but in itself. To will is to delight in willing – it is in Descartes' terms, 'the greatest of contentments'. So it goes with the relation to one's own life. Ultimately there is no final argument as to why one mode of life should be preferred to another or why one kind of action should be preferred to another. One of the most compelling reasons for anything is that it gives contentment and joy in itself while not harming others. And one of the most compelling reasons for the thoughtful self to act is that it is a thoughtful political act, is part of the practice of the civic virtues, is an act of deep citizenship and brings joy or contentment in its own right. It would not be right for such an act to be wanton or unduly harmful. *Politizare* must be both bounded and protected.

This is the point at which politics meets statecraft in a contemporary context.

In Chapter 4 I pointed out that Carl Schmitt had argued that the modern state depends on politics which precedes it. This assumes that the modern state is non-political, a conclusion which, following Machiavelli, it is not hard to reach. Once politics is conceived, *contra* Arendt, as taking place in the social, then the state can either ignore that development, attempt to prevent or limit it or foster it. I have argued that politics, conceived in the sense given it by Dante, is a good in its own right and that taking responsibility for parts of one's own life and taking a share in the conditions of that life needs no further justification.

In any case where the state views empowerment, individual responsibility, autonomy and personal responsibility as goods, it would be perfectly reasonable to expect the state to act in a way that fosters non-statist politics. As the current language of liberal democratic states is charged with these terms it would be consistent for them to foster non-statist politics and the consequent deep citizenship which follows from that. This treats the state as the ladder up which politics has climbed.

All of this implies a post-liberal perfectionist state. It is post-liberal for, among other things, it accepts that the public–private distinction is problematic in a number of ways. It is perfectionist for it believes that a revitalised politics with its civic virtues, deep citizenship and action that is oriented towards the universal (even while rooted in real living) is a good in itself and a good to be fostered.

This splits the activities of the state into a number of separate but related kinds. First, the state is perfectionist but in an open-textured way, viewing *politizare* as a good. Second, the state protects political society in the way that it has classically protected civil society. Third, the state is pro-active in protecting political spaces. Fourth, it accepts and fosters non-statist political activity while not prescribing its content. Fifth, the state provides the framework within which new political spaces can emerge but does not itself create or control such spaces. The state is, however, active in attempting to ensure that everyone is granted the opportunity to and encouraged to engage in appropriate political activity. It is conducive to political activity as *politizare* and it ensures that all its members are stake-holders in political society.

None of these *desiderata* are possible if reasonable criteria of social justice are lacking and if the conditions within which a meaningful degree of autonomy, citizenship and *politizare* cannot be met. All of these require a wide range of social experience and will, in some cases, require the state to be pro-active in the development of meaningful programmes that widen mental horizons. This includes providing individuals with the minimal conditions within which the civic virtues can be exercised, and in providing the education required for civic development.

Meeting these objectives almost certainly requires the state to be pro-active with respect to welfare conditions, for instance welfare responsibilities, some welfare rights, welfare benefits and welfare costs. If the function of the state is to educate people for autonomy, for politics and for deep citizenship it can hardly expect the poor, the deprived, the ignorant, the ill-educated, the alienated, the drug addict, the illegal immigrant, their native-born children, the estranged, the fearful, the frightened, the distressed, the disturbed, the worried and countless other non-stakeholders to do this by themselves. A sense of belonging, a sense of stake-holding does not fall from heaven. If it is acquired at all it is acquired with great difficulty and at considerable social cost. But if the function of the state is to lift the population to a point where they have the opportunity of enjoying a political life, then the cost is just that – the cost. Regarded in this way the state is the commission of and by society to improve society and its members and lift it to new heights. The principle is well recognised in liberalism and is contained in the rousing words of John Stuart Mill when he regards humanity as progressive: it is liberalism's unfulfilled promise, a promise which is not radical in itself but a potential contained within it and which would be radical if actually met.

The failure to meet the promise of liberalism does not imply that there has been no change in either the perception of individuals and individuality or in the structure and remit of the modern state. On the contrary, the trends in changes to the nature of the state are quite widespread. It is clearest in Europe, perhaps, where there is a Europe of the regions and a Europe of the centre. These two Europes, or more accurately the tensions within Europe, are quite marked and, from the point of view of the development of *politizare* and deep citizenship, quite welcome.

There is a similar relation in the United States in the tension between states' rights and federal government. It is also emerging as a consequence in NAFTA which is providing potentially new, economic, social and political arrangements. The much vaunted Pan Africanism, if it were ever to emerge, and it might in some limited sense, and the much talked about relations between Islamic states, Arab states and the Russian Federation, for example, provide a variety of challenges in that they create a tension between centralising tendencies and between separatist or regional tendencies. There is frequently a view that these tensions are harmful and require reconciliation. The argument that I have developed so far suggests that the opposite is the case: the tensions are potentially beneficial and potentially productive of democracy and citizenship in a participatory and not in a merely passive sense. The tensions produce spaces and places within which action is possible. Ambiguity is not necessarily harmful, it is often helpful and freedom enhancing. I have argued that the end of all ambiguity would be impossible but, should it occur, it would be stifling.

There are two principal ways of dealing with the tensions, one is through the increase in formalised arrangements and the other is through enhanced participation and an increased sense of stakeholding. These ways are frequently regarded as incompatible in that, on the one hand, proceduralism reduces the opportunities for participation and, on the other hand, participation undercuts or bypasses procedures. Again this is a helpful tension. An example might help. There is a view, quite widespread in UK-based critiques of Europe, that there is a democratic deficit at the centre of Europe. The basis of the claim rests in part on the view that democracy should be both procedurally adequate and procedurally transparent. This is a fairly standard liberal argument. Liberalism, according to Schmitt's critique,[11] attempts to eliminate politics by substituting procedures for 'the political'. In this he is undoubtedly correct. There is a deep distaste in liberalism for agonistic politics, political participation and anything but the most shallow of citizenship models. Nonetheless liberalism attempts and claims to be democratic and it attempts to meet this claim through transparency of procedures.

The argument can be turned around. An ideal typical democratic institution that met the adequacy and transparency criteria would be an institution that did not involve participation or effective citizenship. The shallow citizen might well know what was going on, why it was going on and according to what criteria of justification, but the shallow citizen would not be a participant in the decision making. Taken to its extreme, it is possible to imagine a democracy that is perfectly adequate in all formal and procedural respects but in which no one participated. Everyone knew what was happening and why but no one was taking part in it. Obviously mere knowledge about what is happening does not make for a satisfactory democracy. This is an extreme, of course: it is an ideal typical model.

There is a different tendency, and again an ideal typical model can be utilised. That alternative is to take democracy not in terms of transparency, openness, procedures and so on, what one might call liberal proceduralism, but in terms of participation and involvement: pure agonism. An agonistic model fosters and depends on the act-moment that mere proceduralism undercuts. Writ large, agonism in the conditions of mass society may turn out to be little more than *ochlocracy*: mob rule. Again this is an ideal typical model.

Fortunately the choice is not as stark or bare as this for both the transparency model and the agonistic model can be adopted. This produces some difficulties in formal terms. The two models are not formally compatible for pure agonism produces results that are not procedurally transparent. And *mere* proceduralism does not present results that are participatory. The qualified freedom that is necessary for democracy emerges from the ambiguity, and it is the same ambiguity that permits the kind of participation required for the beginnings of deep citizenship and the growth of the self. The mirror of self and culture shakes and shimmers slightly and as it does so it permits the ethical, political, theological and philosophical space within which decentred individuality can develop. But that decentred individuality, just because it does develop in and arise from its own space, can properly and without contradiction limit its own activities. It can say of its own activities and its own freedoms that it will exercise them within limits that are procedurally expressed. The self can always reflexively decide and without contradiction that it will go 'thus far and no further'. At one level this is to take the Lutheran position and is a position that is certainly respectable and to be respected. At another level it is to admit that the agonism has hit procedural limits, it is to admit that *politizare* is bounded; and that too is a defensible position. To take *politizare* too far is to destroy the conditions within which it is possible. Sawing off the branch on which one sits, intellectual or political or otherwise, is never an attractive or obviously defensive position.

Taking this uneasy position between procedure and agonism does mean living with uncertainty but it is that, rather than more and better procedures to lessen uncertainty, that is the participatory challenge for the future. It is a challenge that is not confined merely to Europe, but extends to all those aspects of the world where one can find tensions between the formalities of procedure and the requirements of participation. The combination of such models requires living with a degree of uncertainty for there is no rule or algorithm that will determine which tendency will predominate in any particular case or set of cases. But living with uncertainties is neither impossible nor undesirable: on the contrary, it is the *sine qua non* of a revitalised political life. But it does not mean living with unbounded uncertainty, for uncertainty can be bounded while still permitting a space of uncertainty. Indeed such bounds are necessary to create that space – all spaces occur against the backdrop of a context. Just as the *polis* provided the context for politics so the new *polis* occurs in any space of bounded uncertainties. The new *poleis* are the multitude of spaces of bounded uncertainties.

It is the new function of the newly perfectionist state to permit, foster and encourage the growth of such *poleis* while not determining their content. It is the new function of the newly perfectionist state to provide the maximal opportunity for members of society to engage in such activity. That implies a significant pro-active educational and welfare commitment. Such a commitment is not to be regretted as a drain on society. It is rather to be welcomed as an opportunity by which society can lift itself to new heights: heights in which there is the possibility for the development of a reconstructed and post-Western humanism.

The new *poleis* thrive on the ambiguities and the openness of new political spaces wherever they occur. That occurrence might be in traditional political institutions, in social institutions, or in any other possible sets of practices and arrangements that are open to politicisation. The new *poleis* permit a condition that is beyond agonism and representation. They are agonistic in the sense that there are a variety of worlds and spheres of action and influence within which people can act and in which they are citizens at a variety of different and often interlocking levels. Such levels extend beyond the boundaries of the state and into the lives they lead rather than being confined to the formal roles that shallow citizenship ascribes to them. They are representative in that the more inclusive the 'world'(s) in which, and about which, action is required, the more some kind of representation is required. But that representation need not, and indeed must not, be by elected representatives or by states alone. It might be also by other bodies such as single issue groups, groups concerned with environmental matters, protest groups or whatever.

This new political condition, a condition that lies beyond agonism and representation, is not so easily de-politicised as the state might often wish. It is characteristic of that novel, radical form of citizenship that I have called deep citizenship. It covers a form of political action that is likely to grow more than it is likely to diminish and which is irretrievably caught up in the demands for personal identity and integrity, autonomy, mutuality and social and political responsibility. It is reasonable to regard such concerns as a central part of a perfectionist programme of the modern post-liberal state and to expect appropriate public policies. It is also reasonable for the state to support and encourage the activities available to reconstructed, decentred and modern individuals as they act in the new *poleis*.

7

Rethinking Citizenship

I started by suggesting that the world into which we are moving is fractured in multiple ways, that its meta-narratives have collapsed, that its old ideologies have fallen into disrepute and that its old certainties have been transformed into new uncertainties. I suggested that the much heralded end of history was the end of history only in the restricted sense of being the end of a particular history. The end of that hegemonic perspective on history did not end all history; rather, it brought about the commencement of a variety of histories. This has brought with it a multitude of diverse voices into the world(s), each of which appears to have a claim to be heard. This is the start of a new ethico-political variety which brings with it the commencement of politics. What occurred after the end of Babel appears less as a disaster and more as an opportunity. The existence of different voices and different languages is not a source of despair, it is source of a vitalised humanity; it may even be characteristic of a full conception of humanity. Such a vitalised, and not falsely universalised, humanity leaves in its wake the possibility and revitalisation of politics and ethics. Politics is at its worst when there is a single voice and at its best when there are a multitude of voices in a forum where each can be heard. If we live at the commencement of histories we also live at points of ethico-political openness.

That ethic-political openness permits an open-textured perfectionism. An open-textured perfectionism invites a shared perspective on general form while being agnostic about particular content. The perfectionism that I have suggested is derived from Dante's observation that acting politically is a good in itself, that it is this which brings the greatest joy, and from Descartes' observation that willing brings the greatest contentment. Taken together as acting into the world these ideas are found variously as William of Moerbecke's *polistheuma*, Dante's *politizare*, Rousseau's 'sharing in the operation of one's life', and latterly as Arendt's political action. I have used the term *politizare* as the generic expression of this idea. It is an idea that finds great support in the political tradition of thought and which mytho-poetically has its origin in the moment of the Fall, the moment that is definitive of distinctive humanity, and which, after Dante, it became possible to regard as a moment of celebration and not as a moment of despair.

The good of acting politically has not been possible where politics has been understood in the post-Machiavellian conception of politics as statecraft. Rather, the opposite has occurred and politics has been regarded in limited professional terms – and a profession with a rather poor reputation at that. I have suggested, however, that politics is now decentred and that the fundamental categories which were once thought to relate the category of the universal to the public domain are fractured. A consequence of that fracture is that politics can occur anywhere, even, *contra* Arendt, in the social. If that is the case the civic virtues can be practised within a wide variety of contexts, including what have traditionally been regarded as private or social or economic or whatever. The practice of such virtues is citizenship but as it crosses traditional lines so it is not citizenship traditionally understood: it has a depth that traditional concepts of citizenship did not have. None of this implies an end to private interests. Nor does it imply that a private action is automatically an action of virtue, private or public. What makes it an action of civic virtue is the degree to which, while being possibly private in origin and particular in concern, it nevertheless sets selfishness, sectarianism and sectionalism aside in favour of acting into the universal.

This does not imply that there are no private acts; it may be the case that after consideration the private is regarded as the most appropriate form of action. What is crucial is the formula 'after consideration'. An act that is merely and without consideration private is not, however, an act of deep citizenship.

Multiple voices can be accommodated in a variety of ways. One is in an agonistic framework, the space of appearances as Arendt had it. The other is through proceduralism. It is generally taken that the meaningful and widespread practice of the civic virtues in a proceduralist model is incompatible, for the effect of proceduralism, particularly when accompanied by statist conceptions of politics, is to diminish the effective value of citizenship and reduce the opportunity for the practice of the civic virtues. That reduction would be so but for two points. One is the decentring of politics, of shifting it from its centre in the state to other areas of action which is made possible when, as I have shown, the categories of the public and universal are de-coupled and when the coupling of the categories of the private and universal are admitted as *a posteriori* actual possibilities. The second is that statism shifts politics away from the people, but it does not follow automatically that proceduralism has or must have the same effect. It depends on, among other factors, how it is done, the accessibility of the forums in which it takes place, the opportunities for engaging in the formulation of the procedures and the apparent openness by which the procedures are themselves arrived at. Such forums can, themselves, be agonistic and such forums can be places for the practice of the civic virtues and valued in their own right.

This permits a move beyond the old contest between proceduralism and agonism. The practice of the civic virtues may perfectly well take place in the social arena and cross the public–private domain as that has classically been understood. The fundamental change in the way in which the particular and the universal are related to the public and the private is to admit the civic virtues to wide areas of life: most generally wherever one can act towards the universal, therein lies the civic virtues and therein lies deep citizenship. And that can take place in proceduralist forums as well as outside those forums.

I have argued that the practice of the virtues and the development of deep citizenship cannot be separated from the development of selfhood. I have argued that the self is intersubjectively constituted in a weak sense, a consequence of which is that a component of it arises as an overlay on aspects of experience. That experience takes place in a number of domains, the largest of which for most people falls under what used to be referred to as civil society. That category is now, I have argued, outmoded in its classic sense. Civil society is now better regarded as political society, as a *poliety* and the selfhood that arises in such arrangements is a citizen self.[1] The citizen self is an ambivalent and ambiguous category and properly so, for it might range towards one or other of citizen or self and/or keep both in an uneasy and irreducible tension. Both the uneasiness and the irreducibility are necessary if possibilities for thought and action are to be kept open and the tyranny of single dominant categories averted.

No one should be entirely one thing alone, whether that be individual, person, human being, man, woman, ruler, subject, citizen or self or whatever. At the end of the road on which the mental and social singularities of selfishness, sectionalism, and sectarianism are to be found, lies personal and psychic death. The care and growth of self, world and others in an autonomously chosen and not passively given way requires multiple facets of being. Only thus can the poetry of one's own act-moments be self-written and the mind and self be enlarged.

For the citizen self to write that poetry as a deep citizen requires an engagement with the range of concerns about self, others and world that affect it and which in turn it affects. These three dimensions of self, other and world are inextricably linked together as part of being in the world. Deep citizenship offers an opportunity to take care of all three as care of self, care of others and care of the world.[2] It is not possible to separate these components out completely or to give other than a schematic outline of what might be included in each category.

As a general indication, however, under care of self might be included living the moral life, thoughtfulness, refusal to obey immoral commands of state or others, conscientious objection, high standards of personal behaviour, and striving for excellence in whatever one does, what the Greeks called *arete*.

Care of others might cover and include aspects of and manners of social interaction, what Hobbes called civility and manners and which he seemed to regard as a matter of first importance,[3] social concern and care: education, health, welfare, social justice, as well as professional, management, workplace issues and economic issues that impact on people.

Care of the world can be understood in a variety of ways and at a variety of levels. A 'world' is any relatively self-contained social arrangement or association of people reflexively related to each other by virtue of a similar outlook or interest. A workplace, a profession, a club or society, a group of friends, a pressure group, all constitute a 'world' in the sense used here. But such worlds expand and interlock with other more encompassing worlds. A group of people acting in a professional way might be part of a larger professional grouping; a club or society might be part of a yet larger grouping; a pressure group might have intersecting and overlapping concerns with other groups and with aspects of a wider population; and a nation might be part of group of nations. 'Worlds' are all these and more but ultimately *the* World includes the largest grouping it is possible to comprehend and bring under one rubric, *arche* or *ecumene*. It includes the physical and material world. Matters of concern to 'worlds' range from their own continued well being to more particular but related issues, environmental issues, economic and other issues that impact on the world.

It might be argued that the citizen self would make matters of self central to their concern. There is a classic objection to permitting individuals or members of society to bring what might seem to be their own concerns to the public domain, namely that the public domain will be suffused with private interests and private vice, to return to the Mandeville principle. I have argued that not only are there difficulties with that tradition, there are also good grounds to reject it. There is a strong and noble tradition of thought that believes that a central part of citizenship consists in setting aside private and partial concerns and acting for the common good.

It is, of course, always possible that the citizen self might turn out to be selfish and shallow in his or her behaviour and attitude, and would not act or seek to act in the wider interest but sink into selfishness, sectionalism and sectarianism. There seems, however, no reason to think that this should be more so than is currently the case. If anything the opposite is likely. The present characterisation of society as civil society where all relations are private and not political, or not predominantly political, is an arrangement that endorses and extensively permits the pursuit of private interests. By contrast the citizen self in being neither only citizen, nor only self, is more likely to be able to develop the capacity to see things from the vantage of others, as Kant put it in one of his later imperatives.[4] To do that requires the taking of a variety of vantage points from one's own initial stance. To see things from the vantage of others is possible only if one can see one's self from a variety of stances.

There is another counter to the objection that citizen selves would be selfish. In general terms it seems that the most selfishly concerned outlook comes from those with the narrowest or the least enlarged minds. Narrowness of outlook and perspective has been seen by a wide variety of thinkers from Plato, Aristotle, Rousseau, Kant, Mill and onwards as something not to be desired and even to be escaped from or corrected. Mill even came to place mental enlargement at the centre of his thought when he took for a general condition the view of humanity as progressive[5] and where he understood progressive in terms of the enlarged qualities of mind.

There is an additional consequence that seems to flow from this. If the enlargement of mind and breadth of perspective results from being in a variety of positions on which reflection, with its self-creating and self-critical faculties, can develop, then a single political perspective and a single political position is inimical to self-development and enlargement. Put it political terms it would certainly mean not being, for instance, the prisoner of a single ideology or a single mode of thought. As Voegelin put it, schools of thought are prisons for closed minds.[6] But nor should one be a prisoner of a single political loyalty with an inability to critically examine that loyalty and the demands made on it. Political positions should, therefore, be varied and multiple so that each can be examined from the standpoint of another. In theoretical terms this is not to advocate an Archimedian point or a Rawlsian original position or some kind of strange view from nowhere.[7] It is to live in the world that we find but to live in it in a variety of places and in a variety of spaces.

An intriguing consequence of this variety of spaces and places is that it would be reasonable to expect the state to protect non-statist forms of politics and promote the conditions within which they could occur. Such conditions depend not merely on formal protection but also and most significantly on the enlargement of mind required for *politizare* and for deep citizenship. That enlargement of mind is a central part of Mill's view of man as a progressive being and is not, therefore, so far removed from some mainstreams of liberalism as to be unrecognisable or alien. It is, however, as I advocate it, perfectionist, and it is something for which distinct social and political action would be justified. Indeed it consistently follows from any claims that individual empowerment is a social and political goal.

In formal political terms enlargement of mind is enhanced by having a variety of different political positions and a variety of citizenship options. One way of achieving this is through multiple citizenship, multi-level citizenship and a variety of political loyalties. This is the political equivalent of taking the perspective of others. It may be a condition of tension but is none the worse for that. Dual or multiple citizen is sometimes in a condition of tension but is always engaged in a set of critical rather than uncritical possibilities. To be, therefore, a citizen of a particular European country and a citizen of Europe, is not, therefore, a position that is enclosing or limiting or one that produces ineliminable and undesirable tensions. It is one that is potentially enlarging.

This ambiguity of status and multiplicity of positions which is ineliminably part of the notion of deep citizenship is entirely consistent with the best aspects of civic republicanism and the best aspects of liberalism. The best of civic republicanism is the citizen acting out of concern for the common good and not out of selfish or partial concern. So it is with deep citizenship. That the focus of such action is frequently to be found in extra-statist domains such as the ethical, the social and the economic dimensions of society does not license its partiality. There is as much, if not more, room there for common care and unselfishness as elsewhere. On a lesser scale those features apply potentially to all social interaction and to all created worlds. The best of liberalism is in the recognition of the value of the individual and the individual self. Those values are preserved in the notion of the citizen self and the deep citizen and are not lost in the post-liberalism of the present argument.

Similarly the domains of privacy, intimacy and personal life are preserved. Without these components individuality and individuation would be subsumed to some other domain. Not everything is political and not everything is a matter of citizenship, deep or otherwise. Act-moments always invoke narrative and social originary; they are, therefore, not merely ethico-political, but always contain a remembrance, no matter how buried, of ethical, political, theological, and philosophical components. Consequently it is always open to someone in the poetry of their life to declare that an act of theirs is primarily spiritual rather than political. A refusal to participate in a war for instance might be an act of conscientious objection based on the traditional values of privacy of conscience. Alternatively it might be based on the concerns of a deep citizen. There is no rule or algorithm that can determine whether an act of this kind is a matter of conscience or a matter of politics. It is up to the actor to individuate it as they will, always remembering that there are commonly understood limits to how things may be described and how they may not be described.

Deep citizenship certainly implies that one is a full and active member of a particular state but it is also to show certain characteristics and to engage in act-moments that enrich the social imaginary and the world. The *humanitas* implied here is that of living an actual life which reaches towards universality while not having that imposed from on high. It is a top-down domination that was the failure of the old citizenship and the old *humanitas*.

In the world in which we actually find ourselves there is a tension between the category of citizen and the category of human. On the face of it, citizenship is a quasi-universal criterion, everyone who is not stateless is a citizen of some jurisdiction or other. Yet in practice the universality represented in deep citizenship is an *a posteriori* matter. We find out whether someone is a deep citizen not merely by examining their juridical status, but also by examining what it is that they have done and are doing.

Deep citizenship is always a throwing or projecting into the future. An implication of this is that the actions of the deep citizen reach beyond the formally defined public domain and even beyond the new *polis* right into the social imaginary and beyond into the remaining fragments of the social originary. To act as a citizen is to re-create the actions of the gods in the pantheon, and to act as one who in having fallen from the mytho-poetic paradise is both an individual as well as a representative for all of humanity. The act-moment is, therefore, always for oneself but it is also and always for the world. As such it is always more or less complete but never entirely completed.

So understood, being a citizen is not a matter of stepping out of the household, walking across to the assembly and participating in it. Nor is it a matter of leaving one's trading or entrepreneurial status, regarded as a private concern, and shifting one's attention to some constructed and artificially defined common purpose. Such activities and such purposes did exist and were clear enough in their original terms, but they no longer apply.

To step into the classic *polis* was to cross a clear boundary. To step from privacy into partial and insignificant citizenship requires one sort of judgment. To move from partial and insignificant citizenship to partial and significant citizenship requires another sort of judgment, and to step from partial and significant citizenship to full and significant citizenship requires yet another sort of judgment. There are no clear boundary markers, no clear guides and no algorithms that permit this sort of transition to take place cleanly, clearly and without reflection.

If society is partly political, and not exclusively private, citizenship cannot stop at the walls of the city – it must extend beyond it into the *oikos*. And the *oikos* must be one of the places and spaces within which the new *poleis* are created and re-created. One is not a citizen only when one walks past the ring wall of the city; that was true of the earliest days of the *polis*, but not now. One is not a citizen only when one acts in the polling booth. To be a citizen is to be involved in political decisions at all times. And this is a condition that runs very wide indeed, for to be engaged in the world is to be political.

To understand this aright and to act on it is to be a deep citizen.

Once deep citizenship is admitted in this way it becomes a matter of discovery as to the relation between the categories of citizen and human. These categories are not, as the tradition from Aristotle onwards thought, related either necessarily or *a priori*. They are *a posteriori*, discoverable *and* contingent. What this implies is that they are creatable, and constructable as either different, or as similar, just as we collectively wish. Clearly, as the tradition has it, the categories of human and citizen share a great deal but there are, I think, few claims that they are identical. There are exceptions. When Aristotle said that man was *zoon politikon* he identified man and citizen. By excluding women and slaves he limited all of these categories. By contrast when Hobbes rejected the Aristotelian perspective he laid a basis for distinguishing man and citizen that devalued both; and that has continued throughout liberalism. The liberal human, one might say, is distinguished by being non-political for most of the time and inadequately human for all of the time. Yet if social life has political consequences and if to lead a human life is to lead a political and a social life, then the category of citizen and the category of human are, or at least ought to be, extensionally equivalent in almost all respects. Any human ought to be a citizen. This is merely to say, as Aristotle did, that man is a political animal. It is also to say that no one should be denied citizenship, for to deny them that is to deny them an important part of an emboldened and empowered humanity. There is clear empirical evidence for that observation to be found in the diminished humanity accorded to those who are not citizens.

But if citizenship, especially deep citizenship, is such an important category we might ask what is to stop citizenship replacing notions of humanity with the danger being that a political category is placed above a natural category. It might well appear that there are clear problems and clear dangers in such an outcome.[8]

The problems and the dangers are, I think, misplaced. First, both citizen and human are, among other things, political categories. The category of 'human' might appear to be natural, but it is quite a latecomer to social and political discourse and appears, in a moral sense at least, to be no less a construct than related categories, and narrower and more particular than some. Until this, possibly odd, observation is fully recognised it is possible that little advance in, for example, human rights will be made. Second, the category of citizen appears to be older than the category of human.[9] Citizen rights are actually the model for human rights and not the other way round. Third, the politicisation of categories is important not trivial. Fourth, citizenship, as understood here, does not mean mere citizenship, it means that enlarged understanding that comes from comprehending that we relate to all people as sharers of our common destiny.

This last point is significant, for it implies that deep citizenship cannot be confined to the mere membership of states. States, unlike the early unitary cities, are artificial entities. By contrast, in the contemporary world a deep citizen is multiply politicised as a member of a neighbourhood, a member of a variety of associations, economic and professional organisations, workplace situations and related 'worlds' of common outlook, purpose and goals. A deep citizen is also a member of a town (the traditional bourgeoisie) or city, a member of a state, a member of a block of states, a member of the world community and a member of a shared, but not imposed, world destiny. It also implies that the post-modern state can take and realise its own limitations while encouraging and enabling its members to transcend those limits. The realisation of the original purpose of the state, the development and protection of its people, can be obtained only by the state moving into post-modern mode and producing the means by which it can be transcended.

This is far from impossible. Wherever people share a life or aspect of life there is room for a new *polis* to arise. This reaches beyond standard liberal, communitarian, Marxist and related responses to the problem of the relation between society and self. The citizen self straddles both society and self as a decentred yet important individual who is part of a wider political world that provides a variety of points of lived intersections. This multiplicity of points of intersection, in which a fragmented individual seeking some degree of holism finds himself or herself, is the point of a development of a personal yet political identity that I have called the citizen self. Acted out with care this is the foundation of deep citizenship, a model of political care for self, others and world that is suspicious of traditional and imposed boundaries, and which is suspicious of either the removal of action from its consequences, or the conflation of action and consequences. The former removes action from the world and the wider space of appearances, the latter elides the distinction between action and the world with the loss of both. In either case this is a failure that is likely to be disastrous.

The citizen self is a condition beyond both subjectivity and subjection which contains within it the opportunity of becoming a deep citizen. To do this is to act into and yet change the constraints that appear to present themselves as givens. This might seem radical, and in some ways it is. But to some extent it is also a perfectly normal and reasonable development and outcome of where we find ourselves. What is proposed here takes and builds upon features already present in the world. In that sense it is no more than a suggestion that we rethink what we are already doing. Being a deep citizen requires merely acting into, and drawing on, the social and political changes that have already taken place and turning them to a careful and thoughtful advantage.

Deep citizenship brings these aspects of action and factors of world together in a way that integrates action and world while also maintaining their separateness. It invokes the recognition that the actions that one takes are actions into the world which are not to be artificially cut off or separated from the world by some artificial and external determination that one's actions are, or are not, political. To be a deep citizen is to determine for oneself that an action is political.

The position I offer is perfectionist, post-liberal and radically democratic, but the perfectionism is open textured, the liberalism is recognisable and the democracy does no more than invite the continuation of unfinished business.

I am suggesting no more than a position that holds it reasonable to be engaged and consciously so in the world as part of world creation; to recognise the distinction between self and world, self and others, and self and cosmos, while also being conscious of, embracing, and taking responsibility for the intersection of self and others, and self and cosmos. To be a deep citizen is to belong in the world, to Be there by choice and to take care of self, others and world.

Notes

1   The Death of a Universal

1. Francis Fukayama, 'The End of History?', *The National Interest* (Summer 1989), pp. 3–18.
2. Edmund Burke, *Reflections on the Revolution in France* (Harmondsworth: Penguin, 1968).
3. Edward Said, *Orientalism* (London: Penguin, 1991).
4. *Thus Spoke Zarathustra* (1883), Part One in R.J. Hollingdale (ed.), *A Nietzsche Reader* (Harmondsworth: Penguin, 1977), p. 204.
5. Martin Heidegger, 'Letter on Humanism', in David Farrell Krell (ed.), *Martin Heidegger, Basic Writings* (London: Routledge, 1993) p. 225.
6. Michel Foucault, *The Order of Things* (New York: Vintage Books, 1973), p. 385.
7. Hiram Caton, 'Political Thought for Epigones', *Political Theory Newsletter*, 1992, 4, pp. 179–84.
8. Jean Françoise Lyotard, *The Postmodern Condition: A Report on Knowledge,* trans. Geoff Bennington and Brian Massumi, (Manchester: Manchester University Press, 1986).
9. Alasdair MacIntyre, *After Virtue* (London: Duckworth, 1981).
10. Immanuel Kant, 'Idea for a Universal History with a Cosmopolitan Purpose', in Hans Reiss (ed.), *Kant's Political Writings* (Cambridge: Cambridge University Press, 1970), pp. 41–53. G.W.F. Hegel, *Phenomenology of Spirit* (Oxford: Clarendon Press, 1979). Karl Marx, 'Preface to A Contribution to the Critique of Political Economy', in G.A. Cohen, *Karl Marx's Theory of History; A Defence* (Oxford: Clarendon Press, 1978), pp. vii–viii. Francis Fukayama, 'The End of History?', *The National Interest* (Summer 1989), pp. 3–18.
11. Karl Marx and Frederick Engels, 'The German Ideology', in Karl Marx and Frederick Engels, *Collected Works*, Vol. 5 (London: Lawrence and Wishart, 1976).
12. Radically different modes of thought are not capable of mutually critical engagement for they share no significant starting points.
13. Richard Rorty, 'Private Irony and Liberal Hope', in *Contingency, Irony, and Solidarity* (Cambridge: Cambridge University Press, 1989) pp. 73.
14. The definition is that given by Lyotard, *The Postmodern Condition*.
15. William James, *The Varieties of Religious Experience* (London: Fontana, 1960).
16. Michael Oakeshott, 'On History', in *Rationalism in Politics* (London: Methuen, 1962). For a detailed and persuasive rebuttal of the con-

servative reading of Oakeshott, see Stuart G. Isaacs, unpublished Ph.D. dissertation, *Sweet Spontaneous Earth: Politics and the Moral Life in the Philosophy of Michael Oakeshott*, University of Essex, 1996.

17. Cornelius Castoriadis, *The Imaginary Institution of Society* (Cambridge: Polity Press, 1987).
18. Benedict Anderson, *Imaginary Communities: Reflections on the Origins and Spread of Nationalism* (London: Verso, 1983).
19. The phrase is Oakeshott's. See, for example, 'On the Activity of Being an Historian', in *Rationalism in Politics*.

2 Of Myths, Mirrors and Origins

1. Objections of this kind to notions of citizenship are so rife and so regarded as inimical to the notion of citizenship that in some circles citizenship concepts are regarded as incapable of rescue. There is an excellent bibliography in Mary Dietz, 'Context is All: Feminism and Theories of Citizenship', in Chantal Mouffe (ed.), *Dimensions of Radical Democracy* (London and New York: Verso, 1992), pp. 63–88.
2. As a nation is an imagined community. See Benedict Anderson, *Imaginary Communities: Reflections on the Origins and Spread of Nationalism* (London: Verso, 1983). For a wider examination of the concept of the social imaginary, see Cornelius Castoriadis, *The Imaginary Institution of Society* (Cambridge: Polity Press, 1987).
3. Classic examples of regimes running away with 'reality' are Stalinism, Albania and, closer to home, the Pentagon in its Vietnam policy. See e.g. Hannah Arendt, 'Lying in Politics', in *Crises of the Republic* (New York: Harcourt Brace Jovanovich, 1972) and 'Truth and Politics', in *Between Past and Future – Eight Exercises in Political Thought* (New York: The Viking Press, 1961), pp. 227–64.
4. Accounts of the nature of history and the philosophical issues thrown up by historical inquiry are a study in themselves. Patrick Gardiner (ed.), *Theories of History* is wide ranging and covers most standard views. Oakeshott, 'On History', is challenging and illuminating. For a different sort of account, see Hannah Arendt, 'The Concept of History; Ancient and Modern', in *Between Past and Future*, pp. 41–90; and for one of the most perceptive accounts of the fragmentary relation between past and present, see Hannah Arendt's 'Walter Benjamin 1892–1940', which is the introductory essay to his *Illuminations* and is repeated in *Men in Dark Times* (Harmondsworth: Penguin, 1968), pp. 151–203. For the impossibility of standard philosophies of history, see Agnes Heller, *A Philosophy of History in Fragments* (Oxford: Blackwell, 1993).
5. The edition referred to here is quoted at length in Thorkild Jacobsen, *The Treasures of Darkness: A History of Mesopotamian Religion* (New Haven and London: Yale University Press, 1976), p. 88.
6. Ibid., p. 91.
7. Lyotard, *The Postmodern Condition*, p. xxiv.
8. Sophocles, *Antigone* 499–504, trans. Robert Fagels (New York: Quality Paperback, 1994), p. 82.

9. Karl Marx, 'On the Jewish Question', in Karl Marx and Frederick Engels, *Collected Works*, Vol. 3 (London: Lawrence and Wishart, 1975) p. 68.

10. There is a detailed account of this process in Max Weber, *Economy and Society* (New York: Bedminster Press, 1968).

11. Eric Voegelin, *Order in History* (Baton Rouge: Louisiana State University Press, 1956).

12. See especially Malcolm Schofield, *The Stoic Idea of the City* (Cambridge: Cambridge University Press, 1991).

13. There is an excellent account of this process in Colin Gunton, 'Persons', in Paul Barry Clarke and Andrew Linzey (eds), *Dictionary of Ethics, Theology and Society*, (London: Routledge, 1995), pp. 638–41. For a more anthropological account, see Marcel Mauss, 'A Category of the Human Mind: the Notion of Person; the Notion of Self', in Marcel Mauss, *Sociology and Psychology* (London: Routledge and Kegan Paul, 1979). Mauss's article has spawned a number of critical comments; many, together with the original text, are to be found in Michael Caritthers *et al.* (eds), *The Category of the Person* (Cambridge, Cambridge University Press, 1985).

14. Heidegger, 'Letter on Humanism', pp. 213–66.

15. One of the best overall surveys of this problem is in *The Recognition of Aborigine Tribal Customary Law*, The Law Reform Commission Report No. 31, (Canberra: Australian Government Publishing Service, 1976), Vol. 1. In the context of the liberal–communitarian debate, see Will Kymlicka, *Liberalism, Community and Culture* (Oxford: Clarendon Press, 1989).

3 The Looking-Glass Culture

1. The exact origin is unknown but see e.g. Victor Ehrenberg, 'When did the Polis Rise?', *Journal of Hellenic Studies*, Vol. LVII, 1957, pp. 147–59.

2. The synoicism of such cultures is sufficiently great that it is meaningful to talk of a kind of citizenship, a commonality based on brotherhood in adversity and a sharing of the same meta-narrative. The invocation of the meta-narrative is important in saga cultures, for it is there that the idea of the story or saga is most strongly and evidently displayed.

3. See e.g. Anthony Black, *Guilds and Civil Society in European Political Thought from the Twelfth Century to the Present* (London: Methuen, 1984).

4. A most remarkable example of this is found in the dialogue between Pole and Lupset. I have provided an edited and hopefully accessible extract of this otherwise difficult but important document in P.A.B. Clarke (ed.), *Citizenship: A Reader* (London and Boulder, Col.: Pluto Press, 1994), pp. 83–86.

5. Andrew Vincent and Raymond Plant, *Philosophy, Politics and Citizenship: The Life and Thought of the British Idealists* (Oxford: Basil Blackwell, 1984), offers an excellent overview.

6. Bruni and the Federalist Papers both offer good examples.

7. Especially Hannah Arendt, *The Human Condition* (Chicago: University of Chicago Press, 1958).

8. Robert A. Dahl, *A Preface to Democratic Theory* (Chicago: University of Chicago Press, 1956). Benjamin Barber, *Strong Democracy* (Berkeley and Los Angeles: University of California Press, 1984).

9. J.-J. Rousseau, *The Social Contract*, trans G.D.H. Cole (London: Dent, 1973); Immanuel Kant, *The Groundwork of the Metaphysics of Morals* trans H.J. Paton (New York: Harper and Row, 1964).

10. Base and corrupt, according to Cicero.

11. Who distinguished clearly between active and passive citizens.

12. Edmund Burke, *Reflections on the Revolution in France* (Harmondsworth: Penguin, 1973).

13. The clearest example is Thomas Hobbes, who distinctly removes political participation from all except a few, but it is re-created in some form explicit or implicit throughout much of Western liberal thought.

14. As in the aftermath of the French Revolution.

15. As in Rome or in the aftermath of the French Revolution.

16. Acts XXII, 21–9, and Clarke, *Citizenship*, p. 54.

17. Leonardo Bruni, 'Laudatio' (1403–4), in Clarke, *Citizenship*, p. 76, and in Gordon Griffiths, James Hankins, and David Thompson (trans.), *The Humanism of Leonardo Bruni: Selected Texts*, Medieval and Renaissance Texts and Studies, Vol. 46 (Binghamton, NY: State University of New York, 1987), pp. 116–21.

18. Jean-Jacques Rousseau, *The Social Contract*, in Jean-Jacques Rousseau, *The Social Contract and Discourses* (London: Dent, 1913), p. 175, and in Clarke, *Citizenship*, p. 101.

19. Immanuel Kant, *The Groundwork of the Metaphysics of Morals*, trans. H.J. Paton (New York: Harper and Row, 1964).

20. Immanuel Kant, 'The Metaphysics of Morals', Part One: 'The Metaphysical Elements of Right', (1785), in Ernst Cassirer, *Kant's Werke*, Vol. 7. The translation here is based on that by W.D. Hastie, *The Philosophy of Law*, sections 45–7 (Edinburgh: T. and T. Clark, 1887). The relevant extract is contained in full in Clarke, *Citizenship* pp. 103–7.

21. From the fragments of Solon. Fragment 6, reported by Aristotle in *Aristotle on the Athenian Constitution* and in *The Fragments of Solon's Poems*, in Ivan M. Linforth, *Solon the Athenian* (Berkley: University of California Publications in Classical Philology, 1919), Vol. 6, pp. 135–9. See also Clarke, *Citizenship*, pp. 37–8.

22. Thucydides, History of the Peloponnesian War [431 BCE], trans. Richard Crawley (London: Dent, 1910), Book II, Ch. VI, nos 35–47, pp. 120–8, and in Clarke, *Citizenship*, pp. 41–3.

23. Leonardo Bruni, 'Oration for the Funeral of Nanni Strozzi' [1428], in *The Humanism of Leonardo Bruni: Selected Texts*, trans. Gordon Griffiths, James Hankins and David Thompson, Medieval and Renaissance Texts and Studies, Vol. 46 (Binghamton, NY: State University of New York, 1987), pp. 121–7. The relevant section is extracted in Clarke, *Citizenship*, pp. 77–9.

24. Marsilius of Padua, *Defensor Pacis*, Discourse One [1324], in *Defensor Pacis* trans. A. Gewirth, Mediaeval Academy Reprints for Teaching,

vol. 6 (Toronto: University of Toronto Press, 1980), Chs XII, XIII, pp. 45–9, 51–5, and in Clarke, *Citizenship*, pp. 70–3.

25. Kant, *The Metaphysics of Morals* Part One: in *The Metaphysical Elements of Right* in Ernst Cassirer, Kante's *Werke*, Vol. 7, and in Clarke, *Citizenship*, pp. 103–7.

26. *Declaration of the Rights of Men and of Citizens*, in Clarke, *Citizenship*, pp. 115–17.

27. See e.g. Numa Denis Fustel De Coulanges, *The Ancient City: A Study on the Religion, Laws, and Institutions of Greece and Rome* (Baltimore and London: The Johns Hopkins University Press, 1980). See also Paul Barry Clarke, 'The City', in Paul Barry Clarke and Andrew Linzey (eds), *A Dictionary of Ethics, Theology and Society*.

28. For a fuller treatment, see Clarke, 'Bondage', in Clarke and Linzey (eds), *A Dictionary of Ethics, Theology and Society*.

29. Australian Law Reform Commission Report no. 31, 1986. See also Will Kymlicka, *Liberalism, Community and Culture* (Oxford: Clarendon Press, 1989).

30. Kymlicka, *Liberalism*.

31. Leonardo Bruni, 'Oration for the Funeral of Nanni Strozzi' (1428), in *The Humanism of Leonardo Bruni*, pp. 121–7.

32. Cicero, 'On Moral Duties', in M. Hadras (ed.), *The Basic Works of Cicero*, trans. G.B. Gardiner, Book I (New York: Random House, 1951), pp. 13–15.

33. Maximilien Marie Isidore de Robespierre, 'On the Right to Vote' (1791), in George Rude (ed.), *Robespierre*, Great Lives Observed Series (Englewood Cliffs, N.J.: Prentice Hall, 1967), pp. 14–22.

34. It is reflective judgment, rather than determinative judgment, that Arendt places as the 'most political of our faculties'.

4 The Recovery of the Political and the Project of the World

1. See, e.g. Sheldon S. Wolin, *Politics and Vision: Continuity and Innovation in Western Political Thought* (Boston: Little Brown and Co., 1960).

2. For the development of the view that modern political theory is centrally concerned with the state, see Quentin Skinner, *The Foundations of Modern Political Thought*, 2 vols (Cambridge: Cambridge University Press, 1978).

3. The examples are numerous. See e.g. John Rawls, *A Theory of Justice* (London: Oxford University Press, 1971) as an example of someone following a broadly Kantian line and placing the right as prior to the good. For other perspectives, see e.g. M. Sandel, *Liberalism and the Limits of Justice* (Cambridge: Cambridge University Press, 1982). Contrary arguments are developed by Alasdair MacIntyre, *After Virtue* (London: Duckworth, 1981) and Michael Walzer, *Spheres of Justice* (New York: Basic Books, 1983). For an overview of the issues see Stephen Mulhall and Adam Swift, *Liberals and Communitarians* (Oxford, UK and Cambridge, USA: Basil Blackwell, 1992).

4. Arendt, for instance, makes action the centre of politics and then defines action as fleeting and momentary. See especially *The Human Condition*.

5. The issues are discussed fully in Simon Critchley, *The Ethics of Deconstruction: Derrida and Levinas* (Oxford, UK and Cambridge, USA: Basil Blackwell, 1992).

6. I deliberately distinguish between government and politics here. The argument for this is long and extends beyond what I can reasonably cover here. At its simplest, government might be of insects such as bees, a point that Hobbes emphasised. Politics, however, as I understand, is always a matter of negotiation and discussion. It is always a matter of convention and never a matter of nature. Hobbes recognised this latter point but failed to draw the correct conclusions from it.

7. Such continuity is sometimes held to be a basic function of society. See e.g. D.F. Aberle *et al.*, 'The Functional Prerequisites of a Society', in *Ethics*, 60, January 1950, pp. 100–11. The basic claim is maintained almost as a credo in functionalist theories of society and is subject to the objection that it is a tautology in that it merely expresses what is involved in the meaning of the term society. The critique does not aise from a merely contingent set of circumstances but goes much deeper. There is a distinction between that which is necessary and that which is tautologous that is not always appreciated. It is necessary that a society continue itself. It is far from prime features but is not automatic that societies do this. Some societies pass away though ennui. It might be regarded as a reasonable hypothesis that shallow citizenship reduces the significance of meaning structures and meaningful activity and increases the risk of ennui.

8. See e.g. the essays in Oakeshott, *Rationalism in Politics*.

9. Particularly in Edmund Burke, *Reflections on the Revolution in France*, ed. Conor Cruise O'Brien (Harmondsworth: Penguin, 1969).

10. Charles Lindblom, 'Science of "Muddling Through"', *Public Administration Review*, Vol. 19, 1959, pp. 79–88.

11. I have explored this particular case in some detail in 'Beyond the "Banality of Evil"', *British Journal of Political Science*, 10, 1980, pp. 417–39.

12. C.D. Broad, *Scientific Thought* (London: Harcourt, Brace and Co., 1923), p. 393.

13. D. Davidson, *Essays on Actions and Events* (Oxford: Clarendon Press, 1980), p. 166.

14. The best extended treatment of action and its individuation is by Donald Davidson (ibid.).

15. Max Weber, *The Theory of Social and Economic Organisations*, (trans.) Talcott Parsons (Canada: Collier Macmillan, 1964) p. 96.

16. Alfred Schutz, *The Phenomenology of the Social World*, (trans.) George Walsh and Frederick Lehnert (London: Heinemann, 1972).

17. Arendt, *The Human Condition*.

18. This is not to say that nothing can be said about Arendt's use of the term 'action', but it is to say that it resists the analytic analysis that I am employing in this section of my argument. There is a great deal to be said about Arendt's use of the term 'action' but from a different perspective. It is important not to muddle perspectives, e.g., an

analytic argument employed against Arendt's conception of action and a phenomenological argument employed against, for instance, Davidson. That would be like ships passing in the night.

19. Alfred Schutz, 'Subjective and Objective Meaning', in Anthony Giddens (ed.), *Positivism and Sociology* (London: Heinemann, 1974), pp. 38–9.

20. Ibid.

21. Plato, *The Republic*, Bk. III, 398a. in Edith Hamilton and Huntingdon Cairns (eds), *Plato Collected Dialogues* (Princeton: Princeton University Press 1971).

22. For a deeper and more complete analysis of the technical problems involved see Clarke, P.B. *The Autonomy of Politics,* (Aldershot and Brookfield, USA: Avebury, 1988).

23. From Clarke, *Citizenship,* p. 27.

24. Which Voegelin places as ultimately symbolised in Augustine's Comments on the psalms. The moment is revealed in the beautiful lines from Augustine:

Incipit exire qui incipit amare
Exeunt enim multi latenter

He begins to leave who begins to love/Many the leaving who know it not. (*Ennarationes in Psalmos* 64.2), in Eric Voegelin *Anamnesis* (London and Columbia: University of Missouri Press, 1978) p. 40. Time and eternity, being and beyond, are held in tension in the heart. Poetically, at least, one can think of this as the moment of the irruption of existential.

25. A general account of politics conceived in this way is given in Eric Voegelin, *Order in History* (Louisiana: Louisiana State University Press, 1956).

26. I analyse this idea and its relation to politics further in my forthcoming *Autonomy Unbound.*

5   Between the Public and the Private

1. P.B. Clarke 'Citizen Human', in Clarke, *Citizenship,* pp. 4–33.

2. It is perfectly possible, and frequently is the case, that contests are also contests about which view represents the particular and which view represents the universal.

3. Fragment 12 from *The Fragments of Solon's Poems* in Ivan M. Linforth *Solon the Athenian* (Berkley, Calif,: University of California Publications in Classical Philology, Vol. 6, 1919) pp. 141–3 and in Clarke, P.B. *Citizenship* (London: Pluto Press) p. 39.

4. Aristotle, *The Politics*, in Richard McKeon (ed.), *The Basic Works of Aristotle* (New York: Random House, 1941).

5. Thomas Hobbes's Introduction to *Leviathan*, ed. C.B. Macpherson (Harmondsworth: Penguin, 1968), pp. 81–3.

6. Karl Marx, *On the Jewish Question,* in Marx and Engels, *Collected Works,* Vol. 3, pp. 146–74.

7. This is a serious problem, the roots of which go deep into Western culture, even to its very heart. I cannot examine it fully here but I have

given it a more extensive treatment, including an examination of its philosophical and cultural roots, in 'Bondage', in Clarke and Linzey (eds), *Dictionary of Ethics, Theology and Society,* pp. 88–93.

8. The distinction was not always absolute. Solon, for example, in condemning the rape of the temples, noted that lady justice would seek out the perpetrators even if they hid in the deepest and most private recesses of their own chambers. This may be possibly the earliest reference to the fuzziness of the public–private distinction. See Clarke, *Citizenship,* pp. 38–9.

9. The classic example of non-interference is in the Roman doctrine of *Patria Potestas,* according to which a father has the absolute command of life and death over his son. This held even if his son might publicly outrank him. While the doctrine came to be frowned upon and even fell into disuse, it was never formally ended by the public domain. It could not be so ended for the remit of the public domain was carefully circumscribed so as to exclude private and familial arrangements. See Maine, Henry *Ancient Law* (London and Toronto: J.M. Dent, 1917).

10. Marx, *On The Jewish Question.*

11. Bernard Mandeville, *The Fable of the Bees or Private Vices, Publick Benefits,* Vol. 1 (Oxford: Clarendon Press, 1924), p. 24.

12. Desiderius Erasmus, 'The Complaint of Peace' [1517], in *The Essential Erasmus,* (trans.) John P. Dolan (New York: American Library, 1964), p. 194, and in Clarke, *Citizenship,* p. 66.

13. I am grateful to Lawrence Gilbert for reminding me of this example.

14. Oliver Sacks, *An Anthropologist on Mars: Seven Paradoxical Tales* (London: Picador, 1995), pp. 179–232.

15. See e.g. Julia Kristeva, *Strangers to Ourselves* (London: Harvester Wheatsheaf, 1991), and my 'Bondage', in Clarke and Linzey (eds), *A Dictionary of Ethics, Theology and Society.*

6 The New Polis

1. Sheldon Wolin, *Politics and Vision: Continuity and Innovation in Western Political Thought* (Boston: Little, Brown and Company, 1960).

2. Arguments to this effect abound. Alasdair MacIntyre's *After Virtue* is clear, forceful and, almost, persuasive.

3. Thomas Hobbes, *Leviathan,* Ch. 10. See also Leo Strauss, *The Political Philosophy of Hobbes* (Chicago, and London: University of Chicago Press, 1952) and Michael Oakeshott's Introduction to the *Leviathan.*

4. There are numerous accounts of this phenomenon. There is a good summary of different conceptions of mind in Ancient Greece in Karl Popper and John C. Eccles, *The Self and its Brain* (London: Springer International, 1977), and Julia E. Annas, *Hellenistic Philosophy of Mind* (Berkeley: University of California Press, 1992) provides an excellent overview and list of sources.

5. Charles Taylor, *Sources of the Self* (Cambridge: Cambridge University Press, 1989).

6. I. Kant, *The Critique of Judgement,* trans. James Creed Meredith (Oxford: Clarendon Press, 1952); see also Hannah Arendt, *The Life of the Mind* (New York and London: Harcourt Brace and Jovanovich,

1977), P.B. Clarke, *The Autonomy of Politics* (Aldershot and Brookfield: Avebury 1988), and P.B. Clarke, 'Beyond "The Banality of Evil"', *British Journal of Political Science*, 10, 1980, pp. 417–39.
7. Hannah Arendt, *The Life of the Mind* (New York and London: Harcourt Brace and Jovanovich, 1977).
8. MacIntyre, *After Virtue*.
9. René Descartes, 'A Discourse on Method', in F.E. Sutcliffe (trans.) *Descartes; Discourse on Method and the Meditations* (Harmondsworth: Penguin, 1968); Ch. 6 contains the central argument.
10. Arendt *The Human Condition*.
11. Carl Schmitt, *The Concept of the Political* (New Brunswick: Rutgers University Press, 1976), trans. George Schwabb, and *Political Theology: Four Chapters on the Concept of Sovereignty* (Cambridge, Mass.: The MIT Press, 1985).

7 Rethinking Citizenship

1. I much prefer this kind of designation than the one offered by Etienne Balibar, 'Citizen Subject', in Eduardo Cadava, Peter Connor and Jean-Luc Nancy (eds), *Who Comes after the Subject?* (New York and London: Routledge, 1991).
2. The order given draws on Kant's claim that duties to self are basic and required for care of others. This rather individualistic claim has some persuasiveness about it but I present the categories of self, other and world in the order given without Kantian commitment.
3. The strongest interpretation that this is the centre of Hobbes's philosophy is found in Strauss, *The Political Philosophy of Thomas Hobbes*.
4. Kant, *The Critique of Judgement*.
5. John Stuart Mill, *On Utilitarianism*, in Mary Warnock (ed.), *Utilitarianism* (Glasgow: Collins, 1979).
6. Eric Voegelin, *Anamnesis* (Columbia and London: University of Missouri Press, 1978), Ch. 1.
7. The phrase is borrowed from Thomas Nagel, *The View from Nowhere* (New York and Oxford: Oxford University Press, 1986).
8. See e.g. Alexander M. Bickel, 'Citizen or Person? What is Granted Cannot be Taken Away', *The Morality of Consent* (London: Yale University Press, 1975), pp. 50–4. See also my comments on this in Clarke, 'Citizen Human', in Clarke, *Citizenship*, pp. 3–33.
9. See my 'Citizen Human', in Clarke, *Citizenship*.

Index